DELOS THE ISLAND OF MIRACLES:

HOW DELOS CAN HELP YOU FIND A MIRACLE, BECOME YOUR OWN ORACLE AND CHANGE YOUR LIFE

GEORGE VOULGARIS,
DIMITRA VOULGARIS,
AND MICHAEL SAMUELS M.D.
WITH
INTERNATIONAL FRIENDS OF DELOS

Artemis Books
Penn Valley, California
2017

ISBN 978-0-9645181-3-1
PDF: 978-0-945765-06-3
EPUB: 978-0-945765-07-0
MobiPocket: 978-0-945765-08-7
First Edition Text © 2017 by George Voulgaris, Dimitra Voulgaris, and Michael Samuels
All Rights Reserved

Editing & proofreading by Iven Lourie
Interior book design by Gailyn Porter
Cover Design by Gailyn Porter

Published by: Artemis Books
PO Box 1108
Penn Valley, CA 95946
USA

Phone: (800) 869-0658 or (530) 277-5380
E-mail: artemisbooks@gmail.com
Website: http://www.artemis-books.com

Editor's Foreword

How did I come to be involved with this marvelous book? I met Yori (George) Voulgaris in 1970 or so, when he was living temporarily in Montreal and I lived in the Adirondacks in New York, a couple hours away. It turned out that we had both been at college in Illinois, quite close to one another, during the same years of the sixties which have their own stories, of course. Since I hosted Yori at my family's house for a while, he invited me to come and visit his family in Greece in Mykonos, where he was born and raised. I shrugged this off at first, but after working for a year or two in Philadelphia as a substitute teacher and a taxi driver, I saved up the money for a flight to Athens and went on the journey in summer, 1972. I was scheduled to begin graduate school in the fall of 1972, at the University of Arizona, but the Aegean, the warm, hospitable Greek people, the ancient temple sites and places I knew of from childhood reading of Homer and Greek mythology proved too seductive. I extended my stay and finally, after giving serious consideration to staying in Greece, I returned at the end of the year and began graduate studies in January, 1973. During my stay in Greece, I experienced two major influences: one was the archaeological sites that drew me, as something of an obsession, to the temples and shrines. The other was the family life and pristine beauty of contemporary Mykonos, where I got to be a tourist among tourists, living as the guest of Yori's family and watching the visitors from cruise ships and youth hostel tours come and go in the harbor.

As it turned out, there was an ancient sacred site just next door to Mykonos: the island of Delos. It was about a 40-minute ride by kaiki, a small boat, from Mykonos to nearby Delos. I spent several days there, and this was my introduction to the birthplace of Apollo and Artemis, brother and sister divinities of the ancient times all the way up to the Byzantine Christian era. I was both fascinated and enchanted by this extensive site, a Hellenistic period city that had covered the entire island and, due to the currents of history, had never been covered since around 80 B.C. with any more modern construction! The entire island is the archeological site, and I wandered there through neighborhood streets and paths, into excavated houses of the rich, remains of shops like bakeries and ceramic workshops, and the outlines of temples, great and small, as well as a small but beautiful Greek theatre in the round. Yori had grown up next door and played among these ruins as a child, he had them in his blood, in his DNA, perhaps. Already fluent in several languages, he was studying to be certified as an archaeological guide, an expert on all the sites, the history, and the cultures of the Greek territory. I was the beneficiary of a personal tour of several districts in Delos from Yori. On my later visits to Mykonos, I was to learn from the more formal tours he gives and from one or two other guides whose tours I audited as well.

However, in 1972 I had a very special experience on Delos. At that time, there was a little lodge on the island, now expanded into the visitor center and museum, where rooms were rented out. Yori urged me to stay overnight at the site, see this very magical place at night, and come back the next day on the kaiki, so I did that. This overnight stay (which is no longer available to any but the professional archeologists) gifted me with one of my most memorable moments among the indelible impressions I received in Greece. Several of them, actually. I was warned by posted signs and reminded by the groundskeepers not to go out into the ruins at night since there are deep holes, marble fragments, tripping hazards everywhere, and also, possibly, snakes among the stones. Nevertheless, I walked outside after sunset and stood on the ancient packed dirt of Delos and looked over the city. The sky was clear and filled with stars overhead, the air smelled of the salt ocean and the warm breeze from Crete and Africa. As I looked and listened in silence, falling into something of a trance or a dreaming state, I felt the energy of the city as a buzzing around me and a muffled static or rustling noise like the cicadas but more crackling and electric.

I thought of the thousands of people, as I had learned, who had danced and sang and prayed on this island. And the thousands who had been killed at the end by marauders cut loose by a king in Asia Minor, not hostile to the Greeks but to the rising power of the Mediterranean, the Roman republic with its armies and merchants. I felt that the voices were rising around me, that the air was filled with spirits singing, and that indeed, as I had been warned, the ruins were filled with ghosts and not a place to wander at night. I felt fear, but also awe and wonder at the presence of the dead and their years and years of vibrant life still humming on the island.

This passage in the nighttime from 20th century tourist to witness outside of the time track entirely is certainly one of my strongest impressions from the sacred sites in Greece. I had been to Delphi, Sounion, Olympia, Epidaurus, and of course the Acropolis, the Parthenon, and all had impressed me as power points, junctions of ley lines, or whatever description fits the energy radiating from those geographical places. Only Delphi, in my experience, was comparable to Delos in power and energy; of course, these are the two sites most sacred to Apollo. For myself, I was determined to return to the States and start graduate school in literature and writing. In Tucson, Arizona, I also soon came across an ad in an underground paper for a study group, I answered that ad, and I met a man from a spiritual school that became my own school and an upward-leading path for me. My time in Greece prepared me for this contact; it awakened me and sharpened an undefined wish for connection with a larger world and a dimension of experience outside the confinement of ordinary time. I have to acknowledge that my marination in the landscapes and especially the sacred sites of Greece woke me up to my personal journey in my own life, and Delos especially stirred up and manifested this brighter world for me.

On a later visit in 1998, when I wrote a series of poems celebrating Mykonos and Delos, I wrote this line which certainly tracks back to that magical night in 1972: *The root cosmos calls me back from my wandering mind* Q.E.D., then, as I help Yori and Dimitra and Michael launch this book of theirs, I feel that I am returning a favor that benefited me immeasurably. Editing and publishing this book, for me, is not only the fulfillment of an obligation and a plan 40 years in gestation and development but also the opportunity to open this portal for many others, for you, the readers of this book. I hope that you will visit Greece, that you will visit Mykonos, and that you will tour Delos and bring there your sincere, your innermost wishes for fulfillment in your life. And I wish for you the illumination, the expansion of consciousness, the overflowing heart that I have experienced on this island where the ancient comes to life and becomes alive and new again for you!

Na Pate Sto Kalo
Always travel towards the Good!
Iven Lourie, Editor
Mykonos, January, 2016

Introduction

This book introduces you to one of the most powerful places on earth. There is a mystical island, a magical power place on earth that is so curative it can create miracles and empower you to transform your life. It is an ancient sacred place that made miracles for thousands of years and… still does today.

This is your physical and spiritual guidebook to the island that was destined specifically to make miracles; a place created to make your dreams come true. This book will show you how Delos helps you find and connect with your intimate self and be reborn in your own authentic life terms. Like a magic carpet, this book will take you to Delos, physically and/or in your mind's eye. Then, the miracle will manifest in the quality of your new life.

The Adventure Begins

This book is an adventure to encounter a miracle in your life. Delos is alive, it is like an ancient Greek Daemon or spirit guide who speaks to you, giving you extraordinary gifts and consultation. The ruins bring her ancient voice alive for you, to guide you on this great adventure.

Delos has been asleep for two thousand years. It is time for the island to wake up, to become alive as a power place, a sacred site, and an international healing pilgrimage destination again. Delos is being reborn now. People now tour the excavations, and this gem of consciousness and human culture is accessible to anyone who wants to visit.

Delos is the voice of this book, it speaks to you through its ancient symbols and monuments, and it makes you feel healing energy through its powerful sacred monuments.

What we know of Delos starts from its ancient mythology. In mythology, Delos is the island on which two important gods of paganism were born: Apollo, the god of the sun, and his twin sister Artemis (Diana for Rome), the goddess of the moon. This belief of gods and goddesses, paganism, was the religion of the Mediterranean civilized world before Christian times. Delos, as the birthplace of the sacred twins, Apollo and his sister, Artemis, was a very special and important place in Greek religion, a key place in the ancient western world for sacred pilgrimage.

SECTION ONE

How Delos Made And Still Makes Miracles Today:
The History, The Light And Earth Energy
And The Art Of (Ancient) Delos

Chapter One
How Delos Will Make a Miracle for You

A Story: The Woman Who Heard the Voice of Artemis

She was in her late thirties, spending most of her days and energy dealing with a life that—most of the times—seemed meaningless. She didn't make a bad living, had a cosy one-bedroom apartment, a couple of good friends and a steady job but, somehow, she had fallen out of love with herself and the world around her.

When did that happen? She didn't really know. Looking back, she had tried to spot the moment several times until she realized she didn't have a clue. Did it make any difference, anyway? What she felt, however, is that she definitely needed to find a new source of... something. Healing, empowerment, love, whatever its name was, she had to find it.

Planning her summer holidays, she could hear the Greek sun and sea calling her. Four months later, she was on the tiny shuttle boat taking a day trip from Mykonos to Delos. She had read somewhere about the abandoned ancient city and the thought of walking the same alleys as people used to do 2000 years ago was exciting. Besides, it was a welcome break from her beach-and-bar holiday that, after a week, was starting to turn into yet another routine.

When she arrived in Delos, she nodded "no" to the tour guide standing at the gate, waiting for the occasional stranded tourist. She didn't want anybody to show her around, she had the strange feeling this was a journey she had to take on her own.

Flicking through the book she had bought at the last minute, her eye fell on the Minoan fountain chapter. Why not start from there? She let her footsteps lead her to it and read the book a bit further. It was an ancient spring of water, embedded into an extremely simple yet visually powerful construction, bearing a dedication: "To Nymph Minoan." She looked down at the water shimmering below her and then closed her eyes. How peaceful it was. Her mind emptied little by little and started to wander… A public well, a source of life, under the scorching sun. It was no coincidence. She wanted cleansing and rejuvenation, and there it was. In her mind's eye, at the spring, she saw herself as nymph Minoan bathing, every drop of water cooling and cleansing her skin, body and mind. She was surprised by how intensely she felt this. She felt her vital spark illuminated.

Excited and, curiously at peace with this unexpected state of mind, she knew she needed to see more, to experience more of this place. Next, she went to the tomb of the Hyperborean maidens, the ancient place for fertility. In myth, these mystical maidens came on the wind from the North and helped deliver Artemis, the Goddess of the moon. She sat down next to the stone markers and waited, her eyes closed but still aware. In her imagination, she felt each maiden give her a gift, she saw garlands of flowers made and offered to make her as well a mystical maiden. Each garland seemed to fill her with the fertility of feminine energy. She was surprised to discover she felt, at last, genuinely happy in a strange way. This power place made her experience a sense of charm and fecundity, something she hadn't felt for years.

Her next stop was clearer to her now. She went towards the temple of Artemis, goddess of the moon, the main site of grace and feminine power for thousands of years. As she was approaching, she read that this was the place that reorganized the feminine psyche for women in ancient times. She didn't know why, but she knew she was in the right place, at the right time.

She stood there, thinking. "Who is Artemis? What did people do in this place?" She walked through the old foundations, entered what was once Her temple. Walking amongst the remnants, she found a large flat stone. It was hot and she sat, her mind quiet, her body loose. She breathed in and out slowly while everything was quiet around her.

Then, in her imagination, she heard Artemis's voice:
"Do you remember the memories of all women of all time?"
She said, "No."
She heard a cry escape from deep in her womb, and then felt tears rolling down her cheeks, her body shaking, electric from the top of her

head to the tips of her toes. She gulped, cried, swallowed, and wiped her cheeks. What was happening to her?

She said, "How could I have forgotten? What happened?"

Artemis replied, "I will help you, I will remind you. I will change your moons to mine, make you, once again, a daughter of the moon."

She shook and cried, surrendering completely. She let it all out and then felt relief in the silence. She was emptied, releasing tears until she sighed again and then started laughing. The heaviness was gone from her, she realized she was now nourished and safe. She felt her cheeks against Her breast, perfectly fed, feeling Her hand patting her on her back. She was complete.

She stayed there for an hour. She simply sat at the temple of Artemis and let the goddess of the moon give her grace and power through the stones, the marble, the sky, the landscape. She let the energy and the place restructure her feminine psyche, for that's what Artemis is and what Artemis did in her temple for thousands of years. She felt new passion, vigor, and purity enter her soul.

When she was ready, she headed back to the boat. Her mission there was accomplished.

She left the island deeply changed… Powerful, feminine, sexual, a new woman. She has kept this with her for years. She credits this day and Delos for giving her the determination to change her life and listen to the power within her. Delos is a powerful place to reclaim the divine feminine.

Statue of Goddess Artemis with her favorite animal, the deer in the Delos museum

The Ancient Energies and the Ancient Monuments of Delos Make Miracles

This book, like the golden arrow of Abaris (a seer and healer who healed the plagues in Athens in 6 B.C and traveled to the mystical lands on a golden arrow) takes you to Delos.

First, we tell you about the history and mythology of the island and about how its light, its monuments and its art helped make miracles.

Next, we start by showing you the place where the people who made it walked and lived. We take you on a personal tour of the excavations, into the people's homes and shops so you can see Delos out of the eyes of those who lived there and feel the city become like yours. This is teaching you archeology based on the excavations of the ancient city.

Finally, we take you to twelve power places on Delos where people experienced miracles for thousands of years and show you how to experience your own miracle. This is spiritual archeology, based on knowledge acquired from excavations, ancient inscriptions, ancient scriptures and literary works, and art about the ceremonies performed in each place.

Experience a Miracle

To help you find your own miracle we have taken twelve basic awarenesses or consciousness principles of ancient Delos and twelve specific healing places that arose from them. We will show you how in each place, you can do your own private meditation or ceremony using the ancient healing energy that the place created just like the woman did in our first story above.

For example, the ancient awareness of Grace and Power created the ancient place, the Temple of Artemis, the Goddess of the moon. The awareness of Grace and Power was felt by people in one spot, so they built a temple there for the goddess Artemis so they could worship that energy on Delos. This temple was then the place that women and men came for thousands of years to feel Grace and Power, to access the power of the feminine. Now... you can come too and feel this powerful healing energy.

In each of the twelve magic places, you can take the awareness and use the power of the place to encounter your own miracle. For example, in the site of the Hyperborean Maidens, you can use the energy of fertility, to bring fertility and new abundant culture to your life. We will use the twelve ancient Greek energies and the twelve ancient sacred power places on Delos to provide a scaffold for your powerful life change experience and recharge.

This way of using the awareness of consciousness and the place together, is a primordial way of being and is given to us as a gift by Delos. Thus, this is a book about physical archeology (excavations) and spiritual archeology (ceremony, ritual, what was actually done at a site and lived as sensational experience).

By physical archeology we mean a visit to (how to see) the houses and shops by experiencing their existence from excavations. By spiritual archeology, we mean that Delos is an archaeological site but more importantly it was a spiritual center used for sacred transformation and healing. Some of the buildings that have been archaeologically measured, studied, and researched were houses and shops, but more importantly, some also were sacred temples and monuments used for spiritual expression, ceremony, and rebirth.

Delos is now an archaeological site, but it was and is also a sacred place used to achieve spiritual awareness. Generations of archaeologists have spent many years researching and excavating on Delos, and they still don't have all the answers. It is up to us to visit the site, use the knowledge we have, and meditate, thoughtfully, on how we believe the events unfolded. In order to heal yourself you need to put yourself in the footsteps of the ancient people, personally fill in the blanks with your own story and your own life.

We use what we have now, from our present moments of life. For example, if we need all of the information from research to know what a site was used for, what exact ceremony was done in an ancient temple, and we have only a small amount from the archeology research… we need to fill in the blanks for the rest. How do we fill in the blanks in Delos, how do we grasp what happened there to create miracles? The answer is, we go to Delos, we do ceremony, and we see, feel, and imagine. We go to a place, know the myths, the archaeological research and then…try to live it with our lives now and see and experience Delos in our own bodies. We feel how Delos made miracles for thousands of years. Delos tells us how in our gut feeling....

Spiritual archeology is a personal interpretation of what the site of Delos does to people, and what it should do. The interpretation is based on knowledge we have from ancient writings about Delos and from new research by academic archaeologists. We are thankful to the archaeologists who dedicate their lives in the dirt, digging in the heat and the wind. Spiritual archeology is using the excavations, the records, and the given history, combined with our immediate contact with the remnants and what they means to us now. We finalize the experience with our personal evaluation of its impact on us.

The times of only just knowing what the physical site is are gone and past, and this knowledge is a given. Nowadays, we must try to understand what the site does to each individual. It is superficial just to look at the stones; they need to be felt. Feeling the human activity in the stones is the understanding and the connection to Delos. The stones will energize you; it starts with a buzzing feeling, the energy running through your veins. It starts with a buzzing feeling when you feel what comes to you by energy of the endless human activity that created it. We want you to wonder what was the core behind all that activity. These broken walls and remnants are the proof of immense human energy, and unlike other famous monuments, Delos is very personal with its houses, its streets and its everyday life touching you. In fact, the remnants of an entire ancient city with all pertinent parts, temples, houses, schools, markets, theaters, hospitals, and so on, are there in Delos.

Delos Consciousness

Apollo is the god of the sun. Artemis is the goddess of the moon. As a consequence, Apollo is the god of light consciousness and enlightened thinking. Artemis is the goddess of moon consciousness and goddess of earth energy feeling. Apollo was the god of the culture of thinking. During the height of Delos, 5th century B.C., thinking was the maximum human faculty, and the love for the culture of thinking (philosophy) went beyond anything else. For Greek philosophers at that time, thinking was more important than eating. Artemis was the goddess of women, of nature, and she was the bringer of the light of feeling. When you combine the light of Apollo and the light of Artemis you achieve balance in consciousness. The most important question of the time was: Can you think correctly? Can you organize the buzzing energy of Delos into concrete, absolute, effective thinking that balances male and female consciousness.

The word Consciousness exists in ancient Greek more as a verb than a noun. It means inner knowledge about thoughts, deeds, dispositions, inner knowledge you have about yourself. It means to know within yourself. That was what Delos was about, people would come to have an array of various experiences and to know more. They came to Delos to become conscious, to go into a world where they could learn, participate in the rites, not only to do religious ceremonies but also to live it, like being at a huge spiritual banquet in which all aspects and facets of life were present. Mythology provided the guidelines to life, one had to be very near to the mythical example to know the eventuality and the solution to things.

The ancient myths were like a school, people would have experiences of consciousness—the consciousness of love, of creation, the consciousness of power. All the ancient Greek words we discuss in each place were subsets of consciousness experiences. The words match the learnings of ancient Greek consciousness. In Delos, you did not know where you would find yourself, you were the actor in the play, you could choose a temple where you could have a consciousness experience, a life changing experience, and a healing feast.

So, we are using an archaeological site as a stimulus for you to rejuvenate yourself, to realize yourself. Your personal visit to each site is the experience. The discussions in this book are based on academic work which stimulated us, and this resulting work is like original fiction, it is our personal experience of Delos, based on archaeological research and old literary sources. Each site and symbol will result in a consciousness—and the last chapter will be the summary of the awarenesses, the whole gift of the "Delos Consciousness."

Chapter Two
What Is Delos?

What Is Delos?

Even though Delos as an ancient island of miracles sounds fantastic, Delos is a real place. It is a small, beautiful Greek island, southeast of Athens, in the Aegean Sea. It is one of approximately 300 islands that form a round-shaped group called the Cyclades (meaning the round grouped ones).

At least for a thousand years before the time of Christ, Delos was the pilgrimage place of the ancient world because it was the birthplace of Apollo, God of the sun, and Artemis (Diana, for the Latins), goddess of the moon. Delos was one of the most sacred sites in the ancient world, and still is sacred today. It is the portal to the white light of Apollo and the moon and natural earth energy of Artemis. Delos is the place where sky and earth, masculine and feminine, come together.

Now, Delos is an island full of ruins, a UNESCO world heritage archaeological site protected and managed by the Greek government. Delos is an island museum (with visiting hours) and no one, except its archaeologists and guards, restoration and maintenance people, live and work there. There are no cities or villages, no cars or shops on the island. There are only white marble stones and the ruins of what was once a fabulous city, shining in the bright Greek sun, waiting for you. Each year, Delos receives more than 100,000 visitors because of its natural beauty, and the impressive remnants of its ancient city, its spiritual history and… its powerful sacred healing energy.

Delos, now, in addition to being an archaeological site, is an active modern spiritual site of pilgrimage. People come to the ruined temples with their life as an offering to perform ceremony and pray for life change. Like other world class ancient sacred sites, Stonehenge, Angkor Wat, or Machu Pichu, people come here intentionally to find and connect with the ancient secrets that caused life change and miracles in ancient times. They come, become magnetized by certain spots, pray and perform ceremonies to find the present secrets to their personal relationships, to understand who they are, and to immerse themselves into the cosmic energy. You will like the atmosphere, you will love how it makes you feel, and you will realize how the place is a miracle in itself now. Delos is simply one of the most powerful places on earth and this book is your key to how to use it.

A Story: Delos Makes Dreams Come True

He knew Delos for as long as he could remember. His parents, back then a young Italian couple who loved visiting Greece, had taken him there when he was only five years old. He had no specific memories of that first trip to Greece. If you asked him, he couldn't really tell where they went, what they ate, who they met... But there was something he always carried with him. It was an image of himself walking around the marble stones in the bright Greek light. Along with that, came the memory of a feeling. He did not know why, but he could recall he loved it there. The place was strangely familiar to him, it was almost like he had been there before. There, he felt at home.

Every time he would think of the island, the same sensation always came to him: As he walked in the heat and bright light, it seemed that life itself was brighter and fuller. Even 20 years later, when he had become an attractive, accomplished young businessman, constantly moving around the globe, he found himself returning to Delos again and again. Without thought, he came back when he yearned, when he felt something was missing in his life. When he was empty, Delos filled him; when he cried, Delos wiped away his tears.

What he considered to be his utmost dream was becoming CEO for the company he had been working for. He already had a powerful position there, but still knew he could do even better. Focused and determined as he was, he put all his strength into his career and, not too many years later, he managed to get what he wanted. He even brought his executives to Delos so that they could share and understand his worldview, as much as possible. He was certain he knew the island by heart, he could go up and down its hills, walk on its alleys blindfolded, and his enthusiasm easily rubbed off on everybody around him. Without words, Delos did its work with his life. He knew somehow that it was the place where he learned to keep on restructuring his whole reality.

Some years after his big achievement, he decided to visit the island on one of his long weekend trips. Wandering around the ancient ruins once more, he walked past the grave of the Hyperborean Maidens. How come he had never stopped to look at it closely before? It was a curious semi-circular construction. There and then seemed the right moment to explore it. He walked along its stones, watching his feet take one step after another, slowly. Then, he entered what appeared to be a shrine and stood there, trying to visualize what this place meant to those who visited it thousands of years ago. He could sense it was a special meeting point, where people came in search of something. But what could that be?

Back at the hotel, he decided to do a bit of research and see what the sensation that got him so perplexed really was. According to what he read, the Hyperborean Maidens were a powerful symbol of fertility and marriage, especially worshipped on the island of Delos, as the maidens who helped deliver the god Apollo. At their grave, young women and men came and cut a lock of their hair as an offering before getting married and having children. "How curious," he thought. "What does all this have to do with me?"

He went back the next day trying to figure out what was the island's message to him. Up to the previous day, he thought he had managed to get everything he would ever need: a great career, recognition, money, a rich lifestyle. But was that true? Was that all he was worthy of having? Most of it was material possessions or the means to get to them. Looking at the grave, then, he knew. He realized what he had been missing in his busy life. Beyond his work, his career, his success, he wanted to be married and have a family. Before coming back to his Delos, he had not realized that he was so caught up in the rush of his projects and schedules, he did not pause to listen to his soul, to listen to his heart, to listen to himself. Now he understood he had to recover that long-forgotten, buried desire and give a new turn to his life.

Later that same year, he came back to Delos with his fiancée and was married in Mykonos, within sight of the beautiful transformative island. Now, later he takes his wife and children to play in the marble stones under the hot sun. No doubt, it had changed his life forever.

Delos has always been measured by its effects on people's lives. Sometimes the changes are dramatic miracles such as healing from illness, and sometimes softer, like the man realizing he wanted to be married and the marriage happening. The miracles are not handouts, experienced passively, they are actively sought by the person. Each miracle is different, and very intense. Delos is full of stories, ancient and new; stories of lives lost and found, of lives and whole cultures changed forever. That was the miracle of Delos in ancient times and it is still the miracle of Delos today. From a personal level to a global level, the influence of Delos can be profound.

You Don't Have to Visit Delos to Feel a Miracle

Even if you never come to Delos physically, Delos can affect your life. This book is both a guide to create an inner journey in your imagination and a guide book to tour Delos. Delos is so powerful that it can affect you wherever you are on earth. The healing energy of Delos is beyond time and place, it also exists in spirit space for eternity. All energy is most powerful at its source. Delos is most powerful if you are there, but its power goes beyond time and space to reach you now.

If we claim this is a living planet, Delos is one of its self-balancing and healing organs (homeostatic). The healing power of the white light of Delos and its magnetic earth energy balance your higher consciousness and lower consciousness. When you picture Delos in your mind's eye, you can perceive this energy coming to you, and you are balanced and healed. When you picture an energy like fertility and a place like the Tomb of the Hyperborean maidens and its ancient story, you are there in your imagination and the healing energy of Delos fills you. When you picture creation in your imagination, you are working with your energy of creating new beginnings in your life, whether you are in Delos, or reading this book on your couch at home.

Imagining Delos is about embodying the ancient Greek teachings of Apollo—light, and Artemis—nature/earth/moon. Also it will give you a deep first hand insight into classical Greek history and archeology. The age old philosophy of pagan religion (philosophy

Remnants from one of the two graves of Hyperborean maidens in Delos where women would cut a lock of hair before marriage

of science was pagan in ancient cities) can help you find inner light and knowledge. This book is a real tour guide and also a virtual tour, a mind's eye tour in time travel to comprehend the special energy that is Delos. The profound lessons of classical Greece will become available to you as an actual lived archaeological experience. You will become educated in classical history and Greek archeology and exposed to the modern meaning of ancient history. Apollo, Artemis, Pindar, and Plato leave the classics department and become your guides and teachers; ancient Greece becomes alive again. You will experience and become one with the balancing process. This book and Delos will fill your life with the energy of Apollo and Artemis, white light joined with earth and moon energy.

Coming to Delos Is About Creating Sacred Space as a Pilgrim

Real pilgrims aim for a sacred space. Travelers from all over were pilgrims to Delos for thousands of years. This is a destination that is beautiful. Delos would ask its visitors to see the beauty, to be open to the beauty. Delos would speak to them and say, "Look into my eyes and see the beauty, can you see it? Yes you can." The Miracle began with the shift into a new way of seeing, being in the Light, and opening up from within.

Sacred space is coming to life in this experience. When you come as a pilgrim today, Delos becomes alive for you again. The paths become alive again. Each site reveals itself, each monument calls forth the energy within you.

In Delos, you are immediately thrown into yourself, there is nothing you have to come to terms with. It's something deeper, more than just visiting the site. Delos is the trigger, it is an opening. It is a profound spiritual journey to seek a oneness ourselves, to realize the faculties of our consciousness and learn how to use them. Delos opens up our consciousness through traces of ancient ceremony, on ancient foot paths. You walk the ancient footpaths.

What is Spiritual Archeology?

As we said, this is a book about physical archeology of ruins and about spiritual archeology of the deep appreciation for the ruins. Ruins are leftovers of human activity. In ancient times, Delos was the place people came to visit the birthplace of a God and a Goddess. It was a most sacred place to participate in age-old ceremonies and to experience their miracle. So, as an archaeological site, Delos is not only about marble stones, not only about monumental marble buildings, it is about what the buildings were used for; how the beautiful marble buildings were built as sacred places for ceremony, miracles, and life change.

Spiritual archeology is about looking at an ancient archaeological site through the eyes of the people who used to come there, to see and feel what they saw and experienced. We will be your guides to help you experience the same sacred renewal that pilgrims experienced for thousands of years. The concept of spiritual archeology is an important one for this book. If you want an experience for change, performing ceremony in a very powerful sacred historical place, here is an excellent way to do it and have results.

Spiritual archeology is the archeology that attempts to show what happened in a sacred site. It is archeology of ceremony and ritual. It is the voyage in the imagination to see and feel what happened there. It can be done within your imagination with guided imagery (see below) to experience the spiritual life change that was the reason for the existence of monuments and other buildings.

Spiritual archeology is seeing the world—the inside world, when it started, before it evolved into a modern world view. It is a way to see the world of spirits, gods, goddesses the way they were seen in ancient times. In this way, it is an opportunity to experience your own inner spiritual history, to see where you are in your spiritual spaces, to see what you are concerned about, and now... to see it in a new light. People say, "I grew up, I saw who I was becoming, and now I see who I am." History tells us where we came from so we can heal and change.

You need to be concerned with yourself, only with yourself. If you don't know what to do, if you have inactivity, you are not being sensitive to things around you. If you have inactivity and are insensitive—use your senses to wake up. Delos is like a strange planet, a place in the aftermath. You are overwhelmed or it means nothing, that is common when people arrive in Delos the first time. So, start in the very beginning—see, touch, smell, feel, that is the moment you begin to truly experience Delos and what it can do for you. Connect yourself to the place.

In ancient times, the rites of the religions were not separate from everyday life. The stories of the gods and goddesses provided the values and guidelines to make the people's own life changes. Delos shows you in its mythology, the many stories of women, men, life, birth, and death. You find that your personal story happened before. You hear about birth and death, love affairs, war, marriages. In the theater, people would see their own stories acted out on the stage. It was their own everyday lives recast. It was like their own activities were recirculating, it was like information heard from others, like sharing experiences and listening to stories of others.

In Delos, you start with the tools of your own consciousness to help you understand yourself. The structure of this book starts with your consciousness… it's about your senses being sharpened, your sense of timing awakened. When pilgrims arrived on the island, they were taken up by the special atmosphere of religion, the way of life was religious, life itself was a religion in pagan times, day in and day out. It was living and seeing God in everything, all was new then.

Our Stories of Delos and Life Change

This book shares some stories of people whose lives have been changed by Delos to show you how Delos changes lives and can change yours. There are ancient stories from Greek mythology and new stories from people who have come to Delos recently. The stories are used to give you real examples of how to use Delos to make miracles today. The mythological stories are also part of the life of Delos, they are alive on Delos as you walk through the site, the ancient voices speak to you, listen….

Each story of Delos is different. A woman came with her lover. They wanted to experience the energy of Love. They visited the temple of Aphrodite and saw in their mind's eye lovers making love as God and Goddess. A woman came to heal her femininity, she visited the temple of Artemis and saw herself as the woman goddess of the earth and the moon. A woman came who wanted a baby, she visited the Tomb of the Hyperborean maidens and felt the goddesses of childbirth kill her fears and come to her aid. Your story is your own. As you read the stories, see your own path in your mind's eye. The theater, the art, the sculptures (statue in Greek means pleasure/shot of beauty) are all about your own life.

Basic Guided Imagery Exercises for Delos

We have guided imagery exercises in this book to help you reenact the ancient ceremonies in Delos in your imagination. You will see in your mind's eye the city, the ceremony, the healing, the miracles. You will be able to feel them, take them in and be them, whether you go to Delos or picture it in your imagination. More than that, you will be able to find your own ceremony that matches your personal story to find your miracle.

Guided imagery is an ancient meditation technique which uses the mind to change or shift consciousness. It comes from, and is still part of, religions all over the world, from Egypt, Greece, Tibetan Buddhism, Christian/Judaic/Muslim, and from Hinduism. It is used to deepen the experience of prayer and ceremony. It is now used in hospitals, cancer centers, and surgery units worldwide to help healing. It is used to actually energize your your inner world, your visionary space, to heal and to move energy in your body. Almost every cancer center in America has a guided imagery program to help cancer patients.

Guided imagery is now a basic tool in healing, life change, amelioration, enlargement of point of view, and spiritual growth. In ancient times it was not called guided imagery, it was called ecstatic journeying or prayer or ceremony. It was immersing yourself in the spirit world through prayer and ceremony, seeing gods and goddesses, speaking to them, praying to them for healing and change. In the terms of modern psychology, the trance, altered states of consciousness, prayer, meditation, and guided imagery are all ways you can see into your intuitive inner world and heal and change your body's physiology into healing/healed states. These tools are deep in our culture, we can all learn them, they are part of our way of being already. We all do guided imagery, you do it already when you picture something in your mind's eye, when you picture what you will do today, when you picture a ski run before skiing, or when you meditate to get a creative idea. Many people do guided imagery daily as part of yoga, sports, or creativity.

Here is your first guided imagery exercise, so you can practice what it is like and feel Delos. Just read the exercise and then let it happen, you don't need to do it exactly like it is written. Let it be an inspiration for your mind to travel to Delos.

A Guided Imagery for Delos

Relax your body and take several deep breaths, in and out, let yourself relax deeply. Now in your mind's eye imagine you are in Delos. The light is brighter than any light you have ever seen, the day is hot and you are excited and happy to be there. See the island, see the white marble stones, see the clear blue sky, the emerald blue sea, the mountain and the ruined buildings. Feel the ground under your feet, feel the small stones, marble paths and soft sand.

Now sit for a moment, you can picture yourself sitting on a marble stone of a temple, on the earth in the shade, even on a bench in the coffee shop drinking an orange juice, anywhere you wish. Let the healing energy of Delos cover you like a healing blanket. Let it heal you and make you new. If you have any ideas, let them come, and then release them. Rest in this space as long as you wish.

Now, you are back in your place reading, you can carry the experience of Delos in guided imagery outward to your life. You will feel stronger and be able to see deeper. You will be in a healing state. Each time you do a guided imagery about Delos, you will be more relaxed and be able to go deeper and be more deeply healed.

A Story: The Ancient God and Goddess Boreas and Oreithyia Bring Back Their Love

Arriving to Delos on a hired yacht around noon was their big plan for the day. There was no need to wake up at the crack of dawn and wait for the local shuttle boat. They wanted this holiday to be as relaxed as possible now that John had, at last, retired.

He was a famous pilot, in fact, he had been a leader of a flying acrobatics team for all his life. This luxury holiday around the Mediterranean was supposed to be a long-awaited retirement gift from his wife, but it just didn't feel that way. As much as he remembered himself missing his wife and children while he was at work, he would have never guessed that his retirement would be such a rough patch in his life. He wouldn't say it, but it showed. He felt lost and depressed. Without his all-encompassing work, his relationship with his wife was faltering and things were getting dark not only between them, but in both their lives.

Upon getting off the boat, they met the guide who would take them on a private tour of the island. It was a beautiful summer's day and, despite feeling rather depressed, they made an effort to cheer up and show some excitement. A couple of hours later, after having visited most of the archaeological site, the houses, the theatre, the mosaics and temples, they stopped in front of the place where a beautiful statue of a couple, Boreas and Orythyia, used to be. Although the statue was no longer there, the guide started telling them that couple's story, an ancient myth. After a long walk under dazzling sun of the Cyclades they were already feeling rather tired and sunburned, but they politely let the guide go on with the tale, thinking they would be heading back to the yacht soon.

"Boreas was the purple winged god of the north wind. He fell deeply in love with a young maiden, who was a beautiful princess bathing by a spring. He carried her away and took her as his lover. She became the goddess of the mountain gales and together they flew in the clouds and skies. They had beautiful winged children, the goddess of snow and a pair of heroes who protected people. All of them flew like the wind, like their father..."

The couple did not expect to hear such a story. As the guide recounted the myth, something extraordinary started to take place. Just a few minutes ago, they would have admitted they were having a hard time, in spite of their wealth and all the free time they now had in their hands. Life as they knew it had changed forever and it felt like inertia, like death. But just then and there, something else was happening.... This story definitely struck a chord. They felt like Boreas and Orythyia, as if the ancient Greek myth were their story, in an ideal world. It made them realize the strong connection they still had with one another and moved them deeply. After the guide had finished, they stood there, fixated on the spot, for a long time and then walked to the museum to admire the statue itself.

That work of art was everything they had expected it to be. Yes, it was the way they wanted their life to be. There, in the tiny museum, in front of the mesmerizing scene of the abduction of Orythyia sculpted in ancient marble, John, in a flash, became sure of his own destiny. "I will take my beautiful nymph who I truly love and forever we will fly up into the skies... It is the only thing I need for the rest of my life." The story and the sculpture had grabbed him, taken him away, into himself. He was not desperate and lost; he had a choice and that was how he saw his future, living a happy life with the person he most loved and admired. This powerful, symbolic work of art would be his compass from then on.

Delighted, they sailed back to the island of Mykonos. It had taken them a short excursion to Delos and a powerful mythical symbol to realize just who they wanted to be and enter a new stage of living.

It is an ancient curative process—identification with a story, with art, a statue and a myth. It made them into the statue, he has passed into actuality. They realized their life's plan together. In his imagination, in unconscious guided imagery he became the north wind, took his beautiful maiden and flew in the clouds forever.... In this process the man recognized the story of the god of the north wind, his love, put them together and became the god of the north wind Boreas and his lover: emotional energy, place, healing.

The religion of Apollo and Artemis on Delos was about Know Thyself. The society in Delos had no armies, could wage no war, had no consciousness of war in itself when it was just a religious site before it was financial. You have values. When you lose them, it all collapses. The key to this book is consciousness—it's all we have. Delos awakens consciousness—then we become the oracle of our own lives, then miracles happen and then your life changes. Delos awakens consciousness with its huge energy, it is an experience, your senses wake up, the wind, sun, heat, brightness, and light put you deep into consciousness.

This book helps you imagine a place that was so powerful that visiting it would change your life. It helps you imagine a place that has healing energy for transformation and change, that could help you find your dreams and manifest them. It helps you imagine a culture that was designed to uplift and heal spiritually, to exist so that just by being there, you would be reborn and your life would become new and enriched.

Delos is and was that place and this book introduces Delos to you.

The god of the north wind Boreas flying away with his love the nymph Oreithyia

Chapter Three
The Story of How Delos Came to Be Delos History 101

The Philosopher Who Could Not Laugh, an Ancient Story

In early Delian times, Parmeniscus, a famous ancient Greek philosopher, saw something so dark and frightening that he lost his laughter. From that day, he never laughed again. All of Greece talked about this because he was a very famous figure. He wanted to laugh and couldn't. He did everything he could do to laugh and nothing worked.

The ancient texts wrote the story thus: "Parmeniscus, 'the man who never laughed,' consulted the Boeotian oracle in the dark cave of Trophonius that he might in some way break the spell. The god gave him answer hexametrically: 'Go to mother at home, honor her with exceeding great kindness.' The obedient Parmeniscus sought out his mother, and amazed her by his unusual questions. The effect of all this was apparently to make them both more hopelessly solemn than ever."

Not too many years afterwards, our solemn friend came to Delos, as Aegean voyagers from west to east always did in those days (they had a chance for a pilgrimage stopover). While doing the pious rounds on the island, Parmeniscus worshipped in the Letoon or Temple of Leto, next to that of Apollo. Accustomed to the more knowing art in vogue...he was not prepared for the wooden idol which represented Apollo's mother in this ancient shrine. Therefore on catching sight of the idol his devotions were interrupted by uncontrollable fits of laughter. Leto, Apollo's mother, was the mother whom he had been commanded to "honor with exceeding great kindness."

The statue was wooden and roughly carved, maybe not at all what he expected to see. He laughed and laughed and could not stop. Just as the oracle said, "the mother gave him his laughter back."

This story was told by Plutarch and is very old.... Reliving this story now, almost three thousand years later in the same place, we wonder, what did that man see? What triggered the change of his life point of view 180 degrees? There are theories about his surprise at the rough nature of the carving or the teaching of Leto, the mother goddess. But also it is likely that Parmeniscus (as many pilgrims to Delos) participated in so many celebrations, ceremonies, and observances—that his mood and perspective were profoundly changed. Even this effect may be seen as the goddess speaking to him and telling him who she was and healing him of his malady.

Delos was full of the healing energy of miracles then and still has this ability to change your life now. This book helps you to see and experience this.

Why Was Delos the Island of Miracles?

This is one of the most common questions that people ask. The traditional answers, are: it was a good port, it was midpoint between the shores of the Aegean and Mediterranean Sea. But these answers only apply to Delos after it was developed.

If you go deep, deep, deep, to the time of its beginning—there are no accounts like that. In the beginning of Delos, there was no need for a port, the boats were all small and only a step up from the raft stage, Athens and Ephesus on the other shore in Asia Minor were far away and yet to become important.

So why did Delos become the most powerful healing island, the richest center of trade? (After all, a good business deal is a miracle.) We believe it was because the place is very special. The reason why people chose this barren, remote desert island was its energy, its power to make miracles and heal. People were attracted by the very power concentrated in one spot.

How did this small rocky island become a power place of the earth? The Greek myth of Apollo and Artemis was the most ostensible reason in ancient times. It could be that the first king of Delos (in mythology, the son of Apollo) felt the healing earth energy and used this story to energize the island for its inhabitants. The story of Delos as the birthplace of Apollo and Artemis helped form it into a group, make it a powerful community and caused it to attract pilgrims. Let's not forget that the world was much smaller in those days. Delos as the birthplace of Apollo and Artemis attracted people to the island just as Lourdes in France does today.

But the basic reason Delos makes miracles is that Delos is a healing epicenter; the island is a huge vibrating power place by itself. The mythology of the god and goddess comes after the power, and its mythology flows from the energy spots. The healing earth energy of this sacred site is basic, it underlies any story. The modern story about light, earth energy, resonances and healing art is a modern way to try to explain Delos' mysterious seductive power. This power of Delos is more powerful and basic than any story, it is beyond words; it is based on experience of life change and miracles over thousands of years and underlies all stories, reasons and explanations. This is the secret power the book endows to the reader. And the proof is—Delos is active as a healing place right now, even after it has been looted and abandoned and made into a museum.

Greek mythology and religion explained the amazing power of Delos with the story of the birth of two of their most important gods on it. The first priest of Apollo initiator and organizer of his cult on Delos was Anios, Apollo's son, to whom the god bestowed the power of divination. The king/priest's three daughters, Oino, Elaio, and Spermo, had magical powers to generate wine, oil, and grain, in unlimited quantities and so were asked to supply the Greek armies during the Trojan War.

This is the mythological way to describe the extraordinary power of this tiny rocky island that was seen as a source of wonder and miracle or as a magical kingdom.

The Basic Myth or Story of Delos Is This:

Zeus, the king of the Gods had a love affair with Leto. His wife Hera was very jealous. Leto became pregnant, with the twin gods Apollo and Artemis, and Hera forbade anyplace on earth to lodge the pregnant Leto for delivery. Leto looked everywhere for a place to have her babies. She found Delos, a floating island not on earth, a forsaken place, and made a bargain with Delos to have the babies there. Hera, in addition, captured the goddess of childbirth and kept her prisoner and when Leto went into labor, she could not deliver. Four maidens came from the north to help, from the mystical land of Hyperborea along with the goddess of labor, and the babies were born under the palm tree in the sacred lake on little Delos. Delos thus, was the birthplace of the God of the sun and Goddess of the moon.

This story is key to understanding how Delos makes miracles, makes you your own oracle, and changes your life.

A Short History of Delos

The very very early times of Delos were the times of raft navigation, and Delos being the fresh water supplier due to its lake established itself as the commercial and information exchange in the Aegean Sea.

From deep antiquity (about 3000 B.C. and perhaps more), because of its privileged geographical position, people came to the island. The humble beginning of Delos was a small community of fishermen and merchants who possibly brought with them a primitive Cult of Nature (that of the Mother Goddess) that was to develop into a major religious culture and establish Delos as the most venerable Greek island. As the centuries went by the myth had it that two very important Greek gods, Apollo, the sun god of light and music, and his twin sister, Artemis or Diana were born here. Thousands of pilgrims from the other islands and coasts were coming to Delos to celebrate and many of them to trade as well, under the protection of the god. Soon, the religious and the commercial characters of the island merged, one making the existence of the other possible.

Commercial and religious strength brought politics to the island. It was only natural that every political power would be interested; he who had the upper hand on the island had God on his side (that is, he controlled the sanctuary its riches, and what the god was 'decreeing'), and controlled one of the best navigational and trading centers of the Aegean.

With the expansion of the Greeks outside their own land, Delos attracted the big new international commerce. Around the sacred grounds, the little religious-commercial village started to sprawl into a large city that in a couple of centuries would cover most of the island and the nearer parts of Rhenia. Most food had to be imported from the other nearby islands, Delos itself becoming a city. The population stopped being Greek only, as people of various origins interested in making money came and established themselves on the island. Soon the city became a melting pot as Egyptians, Romans, Libyans, Greeks, Italians, Macedonians, Lebanese, Jews, Arabs, Syrians, Phoenicians, Pontians, Bythinians, Tyrians, Sidonians, Antiochians, Beyrutians, and others, brought along their religions, customs, cultures, languages. Among these people were important merchants, bankers, and shipowners who were handling the big commercial deals of the day. Delos was their base, and in their large warehouses there were products passing from their point of origin to their final destination. In this island's market places, one could find anything money could buy: from Arabian spices and perfumes to great quantities of Russian wheat, to all the best qualities of wine from Italy to Lebanon, olive oils, housewares, art works, ivory, products of forestry, and so on. It was also a great slave market; thousands of slaves were bought and sold.

Delos also had a banking and credit system, and even a stock market/Commodity Exchange. Eventually deals were done, notarized, and paid here while the products were elsewhere. Also the money used was minted gold, silver, and copper coins.

This great economic boom was intensified when, about a century and a half before Christ, Delos was declared a duty-free port. At this point, the population swelled into tens of thousands, an amazing thing for such a small place. The archaeologists still do not agree on the exact number, but it was well over 35,000 inhabitants. Needless to say, it was commerce and not the sanctuary that now led the way. This boom, far from being what Delos needed, brought about the destruction of the island. Its commercial and economic power and importance unavoidably entangled it in the big wars and political struggles of the day. Having taken the side of Rome, Delos was sacked and burned by the armies of King Mithridates of Pontus, a great enemy of the Romans. In the year 88 B.C., the king's ships came, set fire to the city, killed thousands and thousands of its inhabitants, and plundered its treasures. From this great destruction Delos never recovered. Her vulnerability, now exposed, led to more and more attacks by pirates and looters. In vain friendly Rome tried to restore her. The tides of the world politics and centers of power had changed. The great trading routes had shifted from the Aegean to the greater Mediterranean. Religion and God Apollo, grand protector and creator of Delos, could no longer give sacred neutrality. The bustling city was thinned out from about the time of Christ onward, into a small community of fishermen again. Thus, after approximately 3,000 years of intense life and history, the great city became a ghost-town, prey to the plunderers.

When the city was lessened, people, weather, and time (with its consequent changes) took their toll. The upper parts of the buildings crumbled, became rubble and dirt, encased and covered the inferior parts of the city. That is why the ruins of Delos are so well preserved. All during the Middle Ages the island was abandoned except as the occasional refuge of pirates or fishermen or as grazing grounds for the poorer (not land-owning) shepherds from larger inhabited islands around.

Needless to say, Delos was not forgotten, since it had been such an important place. Scholars knew about it because ancient texts and historians referred to it.

More than a hundred years ago, the French archaeological team started excavations in an attempt to give the world at least a partial picture of the island and its role in our past. Slowly and patiently the soil, dirt, and rubble are being removed. And right under them are the ruins of the lower parts of the buildings of the past. It has taken a hundred years to excavate less than a third of the whole community. The excavations still go on.

All the ruins are, as a general rule, left as they are found. Only for reasons of preservation are they touched up as soon as they are uncovered since their natural preservative (dirt, soil, and rubble) has been taken away. Here and there you will be confronted with a bit of modern cement, especially on the walls, some white holding-cement is put around the old stuccoes for support. All in all, except in cases that will be pinpointed, everything has been left as found.

A Fast Timeline of Delos' History, Beginning, and Growth

• **3000 - 2000 B.C.** Prehistoric Times – before history was written, late Stone to beginning Bronze Age, the time of the white Cycladic sculptures. People lived with nature in simple stone dwellings, probably worshipping an earth goddess like the Minoans from Crete.

• **2000 - 1000 B.C.** There are legends of Cretan authority on the island and of organized farming and trading. Delos was most probably an important Cretan commercial outpost. There is a reference in Homer of a first king who turned the island into a food catering hub for the Trojan War. This king of Delos named Anios was in mythology, a son of Apollo and his first priest and oracle. He established the official cult of the birth of the two gods on the island and thus initiated the development of a sacred island protected by its sanctity, intentionally free of armies and defenses.

• **1000 - 88 B.C.** This is a millennium of religious activity, ceremony and miracles that brought in the riches to create architecture, sculpture, and the arts, and turned Delos into an international mushrooming city with a population of over 30,000 people and an arena of international politics and finance. It ended up becoming a complex interdependent society, very much a miniature of ours. The commercial and financing activity grew and grew and Delos became richer and richer. It also found a place in international Politics, being the center of the first truly international defense organization (a type of NATO) in the western world namely the Delian League under the leadership of Athens

Two Historical Landmarks of Destruction:

• **425 B.C.** As the treasure of the gods of Delos grew, along with its financial and political influence over the islands, powerful Athens, for understandable reasons, "purified" the island by having all graves removed to the neighboring isle of Rhenia and enforcing a law that—no one could be born or die there henceforth, thus appropriating historically the political and financial and commercial value of Delos for two centuries.

• **88 B.C.** Delos is burned and destroyed in one day in a terrorist raid, 20,000 people killed and 20,000 taken as slaves by 3,000 pirates/mercenaries loyal to King Mithridates of Pontus an archenemy of Rome. The reason: the politics of the day and looting of an until then un-looted treasure island that was accumulating riches due to its religious state and a personal vendetta between Mithridates and Lucius Cornelius Sulla, Roman general and dictator.

After Destruction and the Present Time

• **100-350 A.D.** Christian squatters live in the almost abandoned and ruined city avoiding Roman persecutions. There is even a reference to the Bishopric of Delos in the early Christian times. Ruins of early Christian churches are found on top of the rubble of the old city.
• **350-1600 A.D.** The island is left with a few goat herders, fighting occasional pirates.
• **1650 A.D.** The French king, Louis XIV, has a keen interest in the Sun God and directs towards Delos the first scientific expedition—thus starting the international interest in the archaeology of the island.
• **1827** Delos is given to the people of Mykonos by the first congress of independent Greeks as a reward from the new Greek nation to the community of Mykonos for its participation in the Greek War of Independence from the Sultan and the Ottoman Empire (1821-1827).
• **1872** The French government, in official cooperation with Greece, started official excavations on the island that continue to the present day.
• **2010** Delos is a UNESCO protected World Heritage archaeological site visited by 150,000 people a year.

The Healing Energies of the Greek Gods and Goddesses in Delos

The gods of ancient Greece can be seen as personifications or archetypes of energy forms. They embodied and carried specific energies for the people. Delos was the birthplace of a male and female energy, of the energy of the light and the energy of the darkness, at a time when this kind of energy was better understood without many words. It was the place of sacred healing and balance of the two energies merged as one. All the gods were worshipped with art, music, dance, poetry, and theatre in ceremony. Ceremony enabled people to imbibe the energy without words, it was absorbed naturally, automatically. That enabled people to embody their self-healing energy as direct experience. It was all done in a place of intense bright light and earth energy which amplified the experience infinitely. The healing miracles were felt like a blast of energy, as a body experience in a power place. Apollo and Artemis together, male and female, light and earth, bring a deep spiritual balance beyond cognitive thinking.

Sacred Pilgrimages

The pilgrimages to Delos were made to strengthen relationships with these two energies in a complex way. The pilgrim came to show respect and appease and balance the forces of nature and its spirits, to avoid punishment, to obey the rules of harmony and bring health and balance. The pilgrim coming to Delos came inside the domain of gods and goddesses and participated in all of this. This divine merging of male and female was what was felt, it was all that was holding together within the island's and life's boundaries; this was, in ancient Greece, wholeness which equaled health. The pilgrimages were expensive and difficult. Pilgrims faced sun, heat, wind, and high seas to come and change their lives. This was all part of the healing process. The pilgrimage involved deep participation in art, music, dance, theater, and ceremony.

The curative power of Delos today comes from the same experience of knowledge of these two powerful primal energies. Visiting Delos, or imagining it, heals deeply by immersing the reader in the ancient eternal energies of male and female, light and earth.

Your Pilgrimage

Throughout history sacred pilgrimages have been one of the most powerful ways of experiencing change, transformation, and healing. A pilgrimage is a special state of mind where you invite a new way of seeing and being. It challenges your sense of self and asks important questions about who you are in the Universe. It is an inner passage to silence and entrance to the unknown and to mystery. It is not rest or entertainment. The medieval meaning of pilgrimage was exile on the earth, you leave your familiar world, enter a distorted sense of time where things are surreal. On a pilgrimage, you keep going and pay attention to all. It is a form of meditation in itself, also freedom from local social bonds that puts the pilgrim in an altered state of being. It is facing the death of self, an invitation for rebirth and a miracle. The pilgrim travels, touches the earth, feels the sea, and in our times, the sky, and leaves home.

Now, as in ancient times, thousands of people come to Delos each year from all over the earth. Again, as before, it is expensive and may be as difficult, and that is part of the healing. People come today as a different kind of pilgrim, as experience seekers looking for something, sometimes looking to heal, to balance, to find themselves and again, to find their dreams. No one comes to Delos by accident, every visitor is called by destiny. Conscious people often leave elated, they fall in love, and a life solution comes to them from something much larger. It was like that for thousands of years and is like that again now. Delos is still a mystical magical island, still the place of miracles.

In ancient times, people came as pilgrims here from far away to give offerings to the twin gods Apollo and Artemis. In the religion of ancient Greece, it was said that when the Gods and Goddesses were honored, they would balance people's lives and create harmony for the community. The ceremony, songs and dances were an experience in enhanced consciousness. It was an exchange. The pilgrims came to honor and give offerings and seek a solution to a problem, get involved, find a healing, and create balance. Besides the temples of its two gods, most gods of the ancient Greek religion were also honored on Delos. Every god in Greece was identified with a different aspect of human life and psyche. On Delos all were represented—except the god of war, Ares. Along with commerce and foreign religions, gods from other lands set up temples and sanctuaries and the sacred island grew in scope and importance. Delos drew pilgrims from Egypt, the Middle East, Black Sea, and all over the Mediterranean, and even established the first Jewish synagogue outside of Palestine. Delos became the common meeting place for spiritual experience in the western/ international world.

It was through the etiquette of religious rituals that tolerance and trust was established amongst the different world peoples; and from that mix, trade knowledge and culture and riches developed. Delos also allowed the beginning of an "international religion" that respected and honored a mixture of many religious doctrines and practices. This cultural melting pot of religions included many of the religions of the world, Greek, Egyptian, Syrian, even Jewish. The inclusion of many religions coexisting in the same city is rare on earth, then and now.

The Art and Healing Ceremony

The pilgrim to Delos was welcomed with a constant religious celebration complete with singers, dancers, musicians, and other fine art performers, by one of the most formidable collections of sculpture in the world, by beautiful architecture, and by one of the best theaters. The celebration started right from disembarkation. Pilgrims were met from the boat by the Deliads, young women who danced and sang and led them in a sanctuary full of temples and altars where they would celebrate.

In Ancient Greece, there was no ceremony without dance and music, a song would turn into a sacred procession, people would join in, offerings were carried and the festival would begin. There were poems sung with music and choirs to delight the gods, it was always new and creative. Mythical narratives were danced, sung, and performed in theater. Masks, costumes, and banquets for the gods were celebrated. Sexual ceremonies, sacred marriages, and ecstasy were ways priests and priestesses could bring people into trance to have peak visionary experiences. Seers and oracles and healers (ancient doctors) would tell people about their lives and about their dreams to heal. This art and healing ceremony was so beautiful and transformative that it would change lives.

Then, after the celebration, pilgrims could buy exclusive products from all over the world, meet important and different people, connect and have fun. It was a true celebration with contests of all the arts, in music, dance and song, contests of choruses, all to decide who honored the god and goddess best. The best singers came to sing hymns to the god and goddess, the best dancers, the best poets wrote and sung paeans to the gods and goddess for a thousand years. People would come dressed in their finest clothes, showing off, with all the beauty they could gather to be the sacred offering to the god and goddess and of course to be seen. When the pilgrim left Delos, he or she was taught by Apollo and Artemis or the many other gods and goddesses, healed and content.

After the pilgrimage, the visitors went back to their homes and like stem cells, changed, not only their own lives but also those within their community with the knowledge given from the gods. They had learned to be conscious of their "problem" and make a new life which would include "it." The rituals were "example solutions."

What were the people doing? They were talking to each other, "Did you see that? Did you hear this?" It was an amassing of personal information. Since this place was a hub, people were meeting others with similar interests. Commerce was the greatest drive but at the same time, technological knowhow was exchanged and from there followed the science of mathematics, law, physics, philosophy, poetry and all the arts, it was an information hub. It took a long time to see all this, endless time, to see the treasures, there were lists of the treasures of the gods chiseled on marble, lists of the assets of the gods posted in the open for the public to be informed and seek to see. You needed to stay in Delos a while, or come again if you were lucky just to see the treasures of the gods. The visit to Delos then, considering travel facilities and time would take a major effort and would last long.

Materialism Overcomes Spirit on Delos

As more and more pilgrims came and business grew, Delos be-came a grand financial center. It developed a culture of sacred art, theater, and music, to promote worship, and a culture of money changing, banking, and trade with shipping lanes to market itself to the world. Delos was the real treasure island. Its treasuries were deposits of gold and silver, offerings, and marvels from all over the world, given as gifts to Apollo, Artemis, and to the other gods and goddesses. Without war, fortifications, or military spending, Delos' wealth increased because Delos was seen as sacred and untouch-able. This brought untold wealth, beauty, and wonders of art; the island was referred to as the world's greatest trove. It became famous and every powerful political figure of the time would have poems written to the gods, and bring statues, gold and money offerings. Naturally the offerings were also public relations' tools of the times. They were also historical art gifts. Visitors would be taught history at its best. When a king would give a statue, his name and fame would be on the inscription along with his relation to Delos, and this would be noticed by thousands of pilgrims and all the import-ant people of the time. It also would help Apollo because part of his consciousness course is knowing history.

As more and more people came to Delos, more and more mon-ey and commodities arrived. Consciousness changed from spiritu-al to material. Shopping was exciting in Delos, every conceivable product of the world was available. The island also had the largest variety of choices in its famous slave market. The slaves were mainly prisoners of war bought by the rich who were either from Delos or visitors. The people bought and sold the best products of the world imported to Delos. It became a place to show off, to be seen, to find the best jewelry, wines, and gold. A recent archaeological deduction of the origin of people/merchants of Heliopolis from Mesopotamia stationed in Delos indicates that there were even silks from the Far East for sale in Delos (the silk route). Raw politics and money attracted a new consciousness and seeded banking as we know it today. At that time, politics was not an important social event, it was the art of manipulating the lives of people. Delos attracted manufacturing, crafts, luxury goods—a stock exchange and a commodity exchange were created, futures were sold complete with credit for expanding commerce. This took hundreds of years to develop.

There came a time when miracles and healing were eclipsed by wealth and materialism; the energy of Delos changed. Jealousy, greed, and war came, over and over again. Twice, Athens invaded for power and money, exiled the Delians and installed new immigrants and colonists. Then came more and more threats, political moves, and finally Delos was destroyed by the pirates/mercenaries of King Mithridates. In one day, twenty thousand people were killed, twenty thousand more taken as slaves, and the city was looted and burned leaving only destroyed buildings and a great quarry full of broken pieces of marbles and building material.

Now for 2,000 more years, it sits as a ruin, taken over by nature. This is one of the clear and visible lessons of Delos: after total human war, destruction, and abandonment, nature does take over inevitably.

Chapter Four
Light Healing and Earth Energy
Change Your Physiology to Heal

Delos Has the Brightest Light on Earth

Apollo is all about light energy. God Apollo is the god of the sun and... the sun in Delos is very intense. How can Delos create such a personal involvement with light?

The first answer is from ancient mythology. Delos is the birthplace of the gods of light. The second is that the light and earth energy on Delos alter your physiology to create change and promote self-healing. This recent theory of how Delos heals is a scientific way in which you can understand the healing power of this sacred isle. Delos possesses two unique natural properties in abundance; it has extremely bright clear white light with a high intensity UV level, and it has earth energy that is legendary. Its important history is the proof. These two properties are indispensable for physiological and emotional change and the possibilities of self-healing.

People have always said that Delos has the brightest light on earth. This light, admittedly, is even brighter than that of the neighboring islands. Locals know this, and they protect themselves in every way against the sun and its radiation, they wear a hat, a long sleeve shirt and long pants. (Warning! Cover yourself when you go to Delos!!) One can study and verify this phenomenon by following the daily graphs of the UV content of light in the website of the Atmospheric Physics Laboratory of University of Thessaloniki. (UVnet.gr.) For most of the summer, the UV level is the highest measured.

This form of white light is healing, fights depression and promotes happiness. In hundreds of research studies, bright light exposure has been found to alleviate the symptoms of recurrent winter depression in many patients. There is an extensive research bibliography on the healing power of light. The mechanism of light therapy may involve shifts in the timing (phase) of circadian rhythms. Light has been found to help cancer, heal skin conditions such as acne and psoriasis, promote wound healing, cure neonatal jaundice, help Parkinson's disease, and address many other conditions.

Light is also known to be connected to spiritual and emotional healing. The Nobel prize-winning physicist Dr. David Bohm writes about "a background from which all consciousness unfolds which is a field of light vibrations." Bohm reminds us that we are all made up of light and that "light is energy and it is also information - content, form and structure. It is the potential for everything."

Many practitioners now practice and write about light healing and emphasize the spiritual or soul development potential of light. Light and color are often used to facilitate personal evolution and colored light is often systematically applied to acu-points on the skin to facilitate the exchange of information among the person's conscious, unconscious and superconscious minds.

Greece has always been known for its bright white light. The god of light was born there, the myth is real. Poets and writers have written about the white light of the Cycladic islands and how it makes you see yourself and changes your life. Lawrence Durrell wrote in *The Greek Islands (1978)*, that he was "Electrified by Greek light" and wrote "The light of Greece opened my eyes, penetrated my pores, expanded my whole being. I came home to the world, having found the true center and the real meaning of revolution." In *The Colossus of Maroussi (1941)*, Henry Miller wrote, "Everything here speaks now as it did centuries ago, of illumination. Here the light penetrates directly to the soul, opens the door and windows of the heart, makes one naked, exposed, isolated in a metaphysical bliss which makes everything so clear without being known." This is what the ancient Greeks called "the light of Apollo."

White Light and Miracles of Healing

The characteristics of the light of Apollo were well known in ancient times. When there was a miracle in Delos, people would say they were struck by Zeus's lightning. It was like a buzzing energy, like an overdose of white light and immersing in the qualities of light. It was as if the buzzing took them out of time and space to a place where they understood that what they saw was real, that in time

Abaton, place of a miracle in Delos.

healing miracles were both real and possible. This state promoted susceptibility and readiness; then – the miracle would happen.

When people had miracles in ancient times, they dropped to the ground and announced it in loud voice for everyone to hear: "I had a miracle, a miracle, a miracle!!" Then, the spot of the manifestation was usually fenced off. These small low stonewall fenced areas were called Abatons, e.g., no step, god's spot. Abatons don't exist only in Delos, they are found in other Greek temples and sanctuaries, but Delos has the highest concentration of them. These were the places of miracles, seen and accepted by the whole community, and they were shown and taught as such to the pilgrims. The bystanders who would "witness" the miracle/change would thereafter go about fanning its manifestation—that is how Delos became known as the island of miracles. In the ancient Greek way of looking at miracles, a miracle was a person suddenly realizing and knowing how to handle his or her life situation. It was the answer to the person's question of what to do to heal his or her life.

Iris, goddess of the rainbow, also had a temple in Delos. There, people could worship rainbows, colors of light. Remember, all the temples in Delos were painted bright and happy colors. The Pilgrim actually saw the marble shine with colors; Iris' rainbow was real on Delos.

Earth Energy

Artemis is about the moon and about earth energy. That is why the myth said that Delos had an extraordinary healing and spiritual energy that came from the earth. In ancient Greek poetry it is said that "The Gods from above watch Delos as the far shining star on the black earth." Delos is connected to the star beings. It is one of the places on earth that can reflect the stars mirrored in the sky. Its temples were placed to act as magic geometric mirrors of the constellations. Delos had an energy you can access from within your DNA. People have discussed its earth energy, its place on ley lines, and its special geology in many articles. Ley lines are lines drawn on maps of power places that can be dowsed and felt and theirhigh energy can be measured. There are many ancient and modern maps showing how Delos was the energy center of the earth, how the ley lines intersected from Delos to other sacred sites in Greece and even from sacred places in northern Europe like Avebury and Stonehenge in Great Britain. There are now modern theories of leylines and power that show Delos as the center of all the power spots in Europe. Since there were ley lines on land there were also ley lines on the seas. Delos was the hub of many of these lines and on Ley line maps, Delos is shown, in the middle of the sea as the hub of ley lines.

Ley Lines from England to Greece

Jean Richer, a professor of literature in Great Britain, has written about an axis of sacred sites in Greece that follow ley lines through Delphi, Athens, Delos, Camiros, Prasaias [Apollo's Temple], the Temple of Artemis at Agra, Eleusis and other sites. He links both the temples of Apollo and those of Artemis. Richer's brother Lucien wrote about the ley lines on the Saint Michael and Apollo axis' where he extended his brother's line north-west from Skellig Michael on the south-western coast of Ireland, to Mount Saint Michel, to Greece. Delos is in the center.

At this point we have to refer to the myth of Antaeus, son of Gaea, goddess of mother earth, and Poseidon, god of the sea. An-

taeus was an invincible Titan who got his power from his Gaea, his
mother, by standing on the earth. Antaeus would kill each person
who came onto his territory. One day, Hercules was challenged to a
wrestling match by this powerful titan, who had killed each person
with whom he wrestled. The goddess Athene told Hercules that
if he lifted Antaeus up off the earth, he could take his earth power
away and win. Lifting him up in the air stopped the earth energy

---

Guided Imagery Experiment:
Readiness and Bringing in the Light

*You can experience the healing power of light right now.
"Bringing in the light" is an ancient meditation practice that
concentrates light and love in your life. When you bring in the
light, you are embracing light energy. Bringing in the light is
done with conscious intent. Close your eyes and perform this.
When you are illuminated you understand your spirit clearly and
your intuition is sharpened.*

*Find a place in your life or in Delos that is sacred for you. It
can be the top of the mountain or the temple of Apollo or Artemis
or any other place that calls you. You can also do this practice at
home right now, you can picture Delos if you wish.*

*First, pause, be content with who you are and with the spirit
of Delos. Now close your eyes. Put your arms at your side and
relax. Open your eyes. Now slowly, very slowly, raise your arms
upwards until they almost touch over your head. Now touch your
hands together at the top. It is as if you are pointing upwards
to the sun's heart. Now slowly bring your hands apart and down
to each side. This brings the light down over you and holds it
there. Imagine the light coming down around you like a bubble
of protection, a transparent membrane filled with light. Stand in
the light and feel its beauty and brightness. This is Delos' sacred
light on earth. When you can see His or Her face in the center of
the light, you are receiving a great gift. It is the God Apollo and
Goddess Artemis healing you.*

St Michael Ley line from St Michael's Mount England to Delos Greece

flow from coming into his body. In this same way, we get earth energy from Delos when we visit and do ceremony there.

This earth energy is produced by the living planet. We are more energetically connected to the Earth than most people understand. Earth energy is a rich, dense vibration that supports you in feeling grounded in your physical body. A lack of earth energy results in feeling light headed, alienated, confused, and not being effective in the physical reality. Many psychologists ground their patients intentionally as part of the therapy, and many people doing integrative healing use methods to bring the energy of the earth up into people's bodies. Many practitioners of earth energy healing use tools to help their patients, such as crystals, herbs, and other things that have specific vibrational energies that affect the human body in a healing way. There are a large number of specific techniques that use earth energy to heal, for example, Feng Shui, Reflexology, Yoga, Aromatherapy, and Reiki. All these techniques use earth energy to heal. Delos grounds you with earth energy by itself.

One has to wonder how people in space will have to exist without the earth energy in the future. Life in the space station is definitely a school, and a way to consciously deal with that problem. One has to wonder about moon energy or Mars energy and the reeducation mankind will have to go through.

Guided Imagery:
Feeling the Healing Energy of Delos

Let the light of Delos be what you need to find your own turning point to see beauty. Delos is a turning point in your life, a moment, a new direction. It is a journey to make meaning of a moment of being, you are there to make meaning of your life as journey. It is a journey to understand the meaning of your life. Delos invites you to slip though the veil and go into enchantment to have a mystical journey of enchantment. In this experience, trust the process. Know that what is revealed to you is the truth.

Make your journey in Delos one with the light. Be who you are and feel yourself as the light's essence. Go to places where you feel your essence shines brightest. The elements in Delos are incredibly primal and powerful—sense the feelings in your body, understand the energy of gods, temples, paths. Feel the energy in your body and let it take you, let it happen by itself and grow. Let the enhanced light of Delos wash over your body and purify, cleanse, and heal you. Let emotions come over you to balance and find your own center. Delos is a portal of revelation. Delos is an experience of healing, grounded in an actual journey.

Chapter Five
Art and Healing in Delos:
The Pilgrimage Is About Art Healing You

A Story: The Gods with No Arms Still Heal Today

A man came to Delos from Texas with his mother and sister. He had lost his arms in an accident as a child. When he came to Delos, he was at a loss. He felt he had no identity, he had lost his beauty, and he thought he was ugly. He called himself ugly, believed that he had no beauty, his youth was lost and he was desperate and so were his family.

He came to Delos to see the sculptures of the gods without arms, white marble sculptures of the most beautiful men in history. Before coming to Delos he prepared, he researched the island, read about it, looked at the pictures in books of the incredible sculptures over and over

again. At night he would look at them, absorb this beauty, the men with no arms, and close his eyes and dream. It was like Delos had reached out to him across time and space after thousands of years, as if time and space did not exist.

When he arrived in Delos, he knew exactly where he wanted to go. He went directly to the museum, and he stood in front of the beautiful sculpture of Diadoumenos, a man with no arms, in Delos. He stayed there for hours. By identifying himself with the statue, he got the statue's energy. Slowly, with the help of his will, he made himself into a beautiful man who was as beautiful as the statues without hands. He stood

The Diadoumenos statue from Delos, a man with no arms now.

and looked, closed his eyes and

looked again. He took off the prosthetics he was wearing, In his imagination, slowly, slowly, he became these extraordinarily beautiful men, Gods really. He became them, he identified with them, they entered his body, changed his cells. He was restructured, he was deeply healed.

When he left, he felt that the sculpture had changed his life forever. He saw himself as beautiful now and felt completely different about his body. When he returned home, he finished university *cum laude* and is now a major player in the computer industry promoting communication software for people without hands. He is an extremely handsome man now, full of confidence and beauty, much admired in his profession and personal world.

The art had changed him. The sculptures were sculptures of gods, of energy, of beauty, of what the best artists in Greece could vision. When the gods were made in marble, they came and they were still there for the man with no arms. This man eventually became a golden paralympian athlete, too.

Art and Sculpture

Delos has some of the richest and most beautiful art ever made. The remnants of the sculptures of ancient Greece and Delos are part of the foundations of western art. The figures are so beautiful they are almost breathtaking and lifelike. The marble sculptures of gods and goddesses, heroes, kings, princes, and beautiful maidens draw you in. You identify with the figures, see your own beauty, and react towards healing. When you stand in front of a beautiful statue, you absorb the beauty and imitate the changes in you. In Delos, you as the pilgrim can become one with the light of Apollo and the feminine moon energy of Artemis. You can become one with the birth of power and energy from the source and with the pure power of light and earth.

In Delos, you find your own story in the art and become it deeply. It's like bringing a thought form to life and having it materialize. You come, choose the hero or heroine of your own life story, and can be changed by the sculpture. Statues are about involvement. You can be in contact with a statue, as in ancient times it was part of the mass media communication of healing, along with the paintings that were exposed as murals on the walls of public buildings. In Delos there existed framed paintings in special buildings that were museums of fine art. People were guided through the exhibitions of the art gifts to the gods. The inscriptions under the statues are a way the ancients are talking to you. It's like a dialogue with statues. You can see who ordered them to be made, who made them, and what they symbolize. Also the mythology behind each one counts very much. It was part of the therapy. The story was the historical, emotional value of the art, and now as fragments, with the weight and wisdom of time, the value multiplies in transformative power. When a story of a sculpture tells of the goddess of nature, Artemis, being connected to animals and you look at the sculpture, you are now connected perfectly forever with Artemis.

Muses in Ancient Greece Were to Heal and Transform

In ancient Greece the muses were the goddesses of literature, science, and the arts, especially orally transmitted poetry and myth. The goddesses who were personifications of poetry, dance, and music were the nine daughters of Zeus the sky god and Mnemosyne the goddess of memory. They were also water nymphs associated with springs.

Traditionally artists invoked the muse before making art. They asked the muse to sing through the artist. The nine muses were usually listed as Calliope (epic poetry), Clio (history), Euterpe (flutes and lyric poetry), Thalia (comedy and pastoral poetry), Melpomene (tragedy), Terpsichore (dance), Erato (love poetry), Polyhymnia (sacred poetry), and Urania (astronomy). However, there were probably three original muses, one from the movement of water, one from air, and the last from voice. These three held Aoidē ("song" or "tune"), Meletē ("practice" or "occasion"), and Mnēmē ("memory"). So to make art, the muses taught the cult practice of how to make art. There is a tenth muse, dedicated to women poets who comes from Sappho of Lesbos, the famous Greek poetess.

Music therapy was used extensively in ancient Greece. The ancient Greeks believed that music imitated the movements of the soul and used it for all kinds of healing and deep transformation.

For ancient Greeks, music made miracles and music in Delos was an important part of how Delos created miracles. Plato wrote in his dialogue *Timaeus*, "...harmony, which has motions akin to the revolutions of the Soul within us, was given by the Muses... as an auxiliary to the inner revolution of the Soul, when it has lost its harmony, to assist in restoring it to order and concord with itself." This profound statement demonstrated how the ancient Greeks used music for transformation. Ancient Greeks used music to treat mania, awaken emotions and produce catharsis, and even heal plague by purification. The Pythagoreans used music to heal every day. They listened to music before going to bed to calm down and have a good night's sleep and have pleasant dreams. When they woke up, they played pieces on the lyre, to push away dreams in the night and prepare them for the day's work. The Pythagoreans knew the link between rhythm and emotions, and gave music as a prescription to heal as needed.

The muses were amongst the earliest goddesses and probably predated male gods, coming from Gaia and springs. Greeks built shrines to muses connected to springs or fountains, or caves. The word "Museum" comes from muse, and the early museums were shrines to the muses.

The muse has also been associated with a woman and falling in love as the source of art. Robert Graves wrote, "No Muse-poet grows conscious of the Muse except by experience of a woman in whom the Goddess is to some degree resident."

So...what does this mean in reference to the sculpture in Delos and the Museum on Delos and this book? The healing artist/artist healer falls in love and makes art to heal the self, others, community, and the earth. The inspiration is the woman spirit that is connected to the goddess, water, springs, and caves and is the source of all goddesses throughout time. So the artist healer embodies the goddess to heal. When you go to a museum of ancient Greek art, remember it was made intentionally to transform and heal you. When you stand in front of a sculpture, you are inside the inspiration of the goddess who actually comes to you and heals you, others, community, and the earth.

So when you visit the museum on Delos, the temples on Delos, feel the ancient muse, feel HER. Close your eyes, go deep and let the goddesses who were the muses and still are come into you, your body, embody them. Let them dance you and open your eyes and carry their feminine healing energy to all you breathe. This art in Delos radiates the healing energy of the muse, the goddess, springs, caves, the divine feminine, and divine feminine/divine masculine in unity to heal. It is intentional. When this muse-goddess

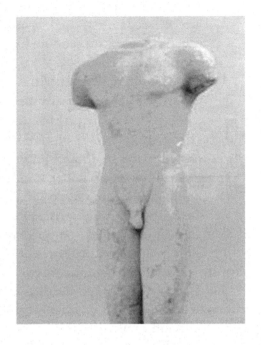

This fragmented statue in its intact form was the perfect example for building a healthy body

of art and healing is invoked in intentional prayer, she comes into your body and you are here—and you too are an artist healer, you are. SHE IS.

The Modern Theory of How Art Heals: The Physiology of Healing Art

The modern story or scientific theory of how art heals, is that a thought, image, or muscle movement changes a cell which helps us heal. It does this in four steps:

1 - The viewer sees the art and has a thought (a poem or play), sees an image (sculpture, painting), feels a dance movement, hears music, participates in creation of a piece of art.
2 - A message is sent to cells all over the body, by a nerve impulse, a hormone, or a neurotransmitter.

3 - The cells become activated to heal. They can be eating a
  cancer cell or virus, sending blood to an area of illness, or
  relaxing or tensing.
4 - As the person remembers a trauma or illness and looks at
  the art, the beauty actually replaces the memory of trauma.

The art changes your body's physiology to heal. Delos was and is
one of the best places of art and healing in the world.

Images made by artists can be so powerful, so filled with energy,
that even though they are not personal to the patient, they too can
be transformative. Throughout recorded history, artists have believed that their images have power in themselves. In ancient times
before Greece, indigenous cultures believed that art could actually
have the power to change the physical world. It was believed to
be able magically to change weather, crops, and to heal. Its shape
and color were believed to be powerful in themselves, to be able
to transmit and move real energy. Just standing near a piece of
healing art was believed to heal. No viewing was necessary, no
understanding obligatory, just an experience that brought about
molecular change. This concept is difficult for many westerners to
grasp scientifically, but it is not that foreign to our lives. People
carry good luck charms, relics, holy objects; people make shrines,
sacred spaces, churches, and meditation rooms. Patients in hospitals today often surround themselves with small altars, power
animals, religious talismans, and crystals. The belief in the healing
energy of objects is deep even in our rational logical world.

Art and healing are now used in hospital programs and cancer
centers worldwide. Delos was one of the birthplaces of art and
healing through spirituality (in the Greek language, the word is
metatopisis, moving from one place to another and changing point
of view). We can still picture this in our mind's eye as we walk the
stone paved paths and see the sculptures in the museum of Delos
today. Art heals by promoting experiences: you see a piece of art,
feel the spirit, have a vision, and the vision changes your physiology, rewires your brain, and heals you. In ancient Delos, a sculpture
of Apollo or Artemis would bring you the light and earth energy
and you would experience the miracle, with dance, music, poems
deepening the trance that promoted it.

Neuroplasticity in the Temple

The powerful images in the art replace old memory images of trauma. For example, if a man lost his arm and had that memory, seeing the sculpture of beauty replaced the memory and rewired his brain with new neural circuits. This is the physiology of standing in front of a piece of art and being healed. Being inside a monument that has consciousness-forming power is learning about our brain's ability to adapt and rewire. This phenomenon is known as neuroplasticity. When you are in a special state of consciousness in the temple, in the monument, you receive the benefits of exercising your brain and building new circuits in new areas. This actually replaces the memory with a new learning and builds new neuronal circuits. You are actually rewiring your brain! This new learning changes memories, heals trauma, and replaces traumatic memory with beauty. It is similar to reconditioning behavioral therapies for phobias where people are exposed to small amounts of what they are afraid of slowly and make new neural circuits that are not phobic producing.

Art and Healing Brings the God and Goddess to Earth

This is how art and healing worked and still work today. People identify with the images they see and picture them in their mind's eye. In the history of art and healing worldwide, it was believed that when a sculptor or painter made the god or goddess, he invoked them, brought them to earth, and their presence could heal. Robert Thurman, Buddhist scholar at Columbia University, writes about this extensively in the history of Tantric Buddhist art. He says that it was believed that the healing goddess, when painted or sculpted, would appear and heal. The god or goddess would be invoked by the artist, and would be made visible in the art, and that way would actually manifest on earth. In the same way, the statue of Apollo could heal as Apollo on earth, the healing god. This continues today in different forms, icons, Hollywood film stars, sports stars.

Delos Was the Center of Art and Healing on Earth

In ancient times, social life in Delos was a continuous ceremony of art events that would change a person's life and heal that person. Choruses came to Delos to sing to the gods and goddesses. Competitions took place amongst groups of boys and girls, young men and women and famous artists from different islands and cities, to see who could make the most beautiful ceremony. People came to compete for the best songs, dances, poems, and theatre. This raised the level of the quality of art to levels unimaginable until then of beauty and knowledge.

There was no ritual without dance, a song turned into dance, into an exuberant procession, people joined in, offerings were carried. In your mind's eye, if you want to, you can see the people dancing and singing and you can imagine the serpent dance spiraling, your energy rising, you can feel it boiling up within you. There were always poems, each time new, to delight the gods. Mythical narratives of dances and songs and poems threw you into the stories, you saw Apollo, you felt Artemis, you saw Isis and the crane dance, you were taken wildly into her energy. There were masks, animal masks, costumes acting out myths, Gorgons, Pan, masked dancers whirling, singing and dancing, even comedy criticizing people handling social matters. There were plays with masked sexual dancing, there were contests for everything. It was a banquet of the gods, a banquet like costumed gods, a Sacred marriage of Zeus and Hera, the marrying of heaven and earth. Greek poets wrote how the young girls, the Deliads, could actually sing so every man thought it was in his own language, this was ceremony in deep trance like speaking in tongues. In their serpent dancing they created ecstasy, trance, you saw and became seers, oracles, they brought you sacred visions of gods, goddesses dancing in love. There was also a very important social "oneness" that was created with the union of the participants. Art always creates community which heals, too.

Vast Treasuries of the Gods

You as the pilgrim could admire great works of art, innumerable golden crowns, the actual whole flagship of a king in a marble temple, There were embroideries, silver work, ceremonial vessels, paintings, and gold and silver pieces galore all accounted for in itemized lists. There were gold and ivory objects, statues of the gods. These items even in a fragmentary state are still sought after as the most expensive art items in the world—Greek art. If there is an art history museum in the world that does not have Greek art, it's secondary. The standards in art were raised by seeing the best art, and paintings and sculptures were symbols of historical events so you learned history with myths, you exchanged information. It was the sacred teaching of the time. Sacred school, initiation through art and identification. Myths were taught and transmitted through theatre, sculpture, dance, and poetry. The cultural stories were told with art. Through art, the stories could be embodied, you felt them in your body as people danced them. The myths were the symbols of real life, guidebooks to speak of, one would never be wrong by following them for advancement and taking heed of their wisdom.

Art for the Gods

In a modern sense, Delos was a great museum of art, it had collected more than a thousand years of treasure amazement. Delos was the world's greatest trove of gifts to the gods. It was all about raising the standards of people toward a personal miracle. Even today, people go to major museums like the Louvre to experience the highest standards of art and have a transformative experience. Why would people make these great offerings if not to work towards a miracle? It was a show of ego, but it was done to make a miracle healing; art was given as a petition and as thanks.

The Stones Have Real Power

Delos is like a great puzzle; archaeologists are trying to assemble the whole from pieces lying everywhere in seeming disorder. After an excavation, the stones pertaining to the monument are assembled around its foundations, listed, and numbered. You can even see the numbers on stones in Delos, but there are missing pieces too. Greek architecture started simple, with buildings made out of stone and wood. We can see that in the older ruins of Delos. We can see the evolution of marble and its techniques that evolved over time, this was not invented overnight. The finished monument even protects itself, once you take away one piece, the whole thing starts disintegrating; every part is an integral part of the whole. When you look at the pile of marble stones, what you see is 2,000 years' worth of the culture of Delos. They made these stones out of marble by hand, with iron tools invented a thousand years earlier. Innumerable marble workers organized in guilds working for hundreds of years, built the monuments in Delos and its city. The stones and their history are like this and you are here now. It is all that time, until this moment is this moment; what you see is condensed time. The stones have power. Comprehend the stones, they carry the human energy behind them. Be empathic, then the stones can work on you and you can feel their power and energy. The stones are alive and full of power, the power of sculpture, of the gods they portrayed. The gods would come with the sculpture and they are still in it.... The god's power is the power of the sculpture.

Morphic Resonance In Delos

Delos also has the resonance of thousands of years of sacred ceremony and prayer. Rupert Sheldrake, British biologist, calls this memory of place and experience "morphic resonance," and says spiritual forms are still alive in places where ceremony was done. Thousands of pilgrims came to Delos and prayed and did ceremony there for over two thousand years. These ceremonies and prayers are still alive as energy forms in Delos now. This book pinpoints and urges you to experience these resonances today when you visit the island by choosing a place where the morphic resonance is strongest and following your guided imageries so you can feel the resonances of the art healing sacred ceremonies that took place there.

Guided Imagery: Stand in Front of a Statue

Imagine that you are going into a temple in Delos. Go inside. Now imagine a statue of a god or goddess in the temple.

See the sculpture of the god, or goddess, feel it in your body, hold your body in the same position for a moment, feel your cells change as you become the god or goddess, as they enter your body and you transform. Stand in front of the statue... imitate its body language... become it.... Once you are in its exact posture, you heal, and something more happens to you: it is statue empathy. You become her, you become him, your body is restructured.

You can also listen to the God or Goddess and hear them speak to you.

(To imagine the different kinds of sculpture people were exposed to, to understand this, it helps to visit the museum collection. There were statures of wood, marble, bronze, etc., and you also can visit the statues in the museum of Piraeus.)

Chapter Six
The Journey Begins—Coming to Delos

Going to Delos is your destiny. Become sensitive, it takes a half hour of just being. You are alone with yourself on a Greek island—you better know what's happening—you are with yourself and your whole life... so... there are voices, feelings, body sensations, buzzing, dizziness. You don't hear voices, you feel them. Delos is not an artificially created world. This world was very real, it had a beginning and it still is.

Delos is filled with a buzzing, healing energy, it takes care of you by telling you how to take care of yourself. There is an immense feeling of now which generates justice, freedom, beauty, that is what heating up and bright light do to you. Know thyself—heat—then you experience what is generated from those conditions.

When You Arrive on Delos...

You are exactly where you are meant to be. Again, it is your destiny to be here. Since you are here, your life has been exactly as it should be—everything perfectly aligned for this moment. You will receive a gift of revelation, because you, as a pilgrim, have found your way here. A miracle will be granted to you in your life. Be very, very, very honest what you wish for, because your request will be granted. A miracle will come to be.

Be awake. Be sensitive. Be alive...slow down...take nothing for granted, so you will not miss it when it comes. There will be an illuminated moment when your heart will open and you will know yourself more deeply than ever before. The light will penetrate your mind, body, spirit like a laser shaft of Light. Stand fast! You may be afraid, let it be, let it go. Inside this fear you are bound, feel your fear...feel your limitations.

Then, the journey begins...walk into the Delos market, you can see how you distract yourself. You may think about your life as it was in the past…as it is now, as it will be from this day forward—everything is possible…in Delos, thoughts and emotions come into the open space of the ruins.

The island will strike you with a lightning bolt, the lions will roar, the priestesses will seduce you. The penis worship is real, the dances, the altered states of being, are all a remembering. Open and let yourself be taken back into the ancient times. It strips you, just let the wind blow everything away for this day, everything you know, everything you are attached to. In this light all your thoughts will be revealed to you. Watch, listen, breathe, put one foot in front of the other, keep walking into the mystery of this power place of the gods and goddesses. You are in ancient times and at this moment.

All of the gods that stood before Christ came here. Since they are remembered, they have been invoked once again. They have returned to grant your wish…. A Miracle is waiting for you here. Watch, look. ponder what it is you are really up to. This Delos moment will manifest your dreams.

Experience the steps of ancient pilgrimage…make your personal ceremony… change your life. Delos does it for you, you do it for yourself.

Guided Imagery to
Go into Your Consciousness

Close your eyes and feel Delos, she speaks to you now 3,000 years later.

Make a clear request for your heart to open and your consciousness to awaken.
Feel the Light and walk the pathways of the Ancient ruins.

Feel the earth energies gently opening your body.
Feel your footsteps re-track into the ancient times bringing back the times to be re-lived in this new spiritual dimension.

Feel the ancient energies of creation, protection, strength, metamorphosis, health, leadership, love, the source of life, power and grace, oracular power, fertility, victory, health, and strength.

SECTION TWO:

Delos As A Physical Experience:
The Archeological Space Of Delos

Chapter Seven
Excavations

Once on Delos you will be confronted with the only thing there is on that small island: its archaeological space which consists of piles of rubble and excavated areas that are really the ruins of what was once a glorious city. These ruins are called "monuments" in the archaeological jargon.

This city was growing sideways and up in its several millennia development period and in its residential areas the buildings had second and sometimes third floors.

This is a collection of broken ceramics, or shards, freshly excavated and washed. The restoration people will have to put together into the their previous intact state as many vessels as they can. Missing pieces are substituted with new material.

Destruction, abandonment, looting, weather erosion, and time turned the upper parts of the buildings into rubble and debris that fell and covered its lower parts thus preserving a good part of the ground floor of the city up to our times.

Basically the work of the excavators is to carefully "shave" the rubble and uncover what is hidden in it. Sieve the debris and pick out whatever remnants or items are in the debris, record all they find, and start stabilizing the uncovered ruins into their new exposed and visitable state.

Excavation is a tedious handwork, and it allows no mistakes since the thread of time which is the state of the ruins must not be violently destroyed but gradually "shaved" with hand picks and brushes, thus allowing the excavator to "gradually unravel" the destruction in a reverse way. This unraveling is meticulously recorded in more than one way, and eventually all these records will be edited into the publication of the particular excavation which presents its history, the gradual unraveling, the finds, and the monument as it was in its original state as closely as possible. Publications like these are mainly the bibliography titles in the history books.

Two governments are involved in the excavations of Delos: the French and the Greek.

Due to its role as the birthplace of the Sun god Apollo, Delos attracted the interest of France's King Louis XIV (who called himself "the sun king") who about 300 years ago sent to this island a scientific expedition with the assignment to report to the king all about the place where the sun god was born. This expedition and many others that followed enriched the great tradition of French classical letters, art, and architecture; and it is, in fact, still going on today as an important formal governmental institution called "the French School of Archaeology at Athens." It organizes and oversees the excavations of Delos along with some other important archaeological sites in Greece. All of France's major universities that have classical departments participate in the excavations of Delos, and every year many groups of archaeology students with their professors enrich our knowledge of Delos' past.

The manager of the site is the Greek government, and it is in charge of the protection, preservation, and restoration of the finds.

The island is basically considered a museum, and it is an entire world on its own. There are people working on it, and these are guards, archaeologists, restoration and maintenance people who stay on the island in the small modern houses that one can see scattered around. There is also a large building that serves as a museum, a storage for the finds, and a laboratory for cleaning and restoring items found in the excavations.

So in the archaeological space of Delos one can see many rubble piles and excavated or "uncovered" parts of the ancient city. There is much, very much of the archaeological space still unexcavated, and it looks to an uninitiated person like normal countryside. How wrong! The old city lies in fact everywhere unexcavated and promising.

Rubble is a great problem to the excavators since one cannot dispose of it. In fact, the pier where your boat docks is made out of rubble from the excavation, and as we shall see later on, the sacred lake was dried up with equally the same rubble.

In Delos the so far excavated archaeological space consists of two kinds of monuments:

A) remnants of public buildings that could be sacred (temples, altars, shrines, churches, synagogue) or civic usage buildings like administrative buildings, market places, theaters, water reserves, schools, stadium, and so on.

B) remnants of the ancient town in a very good state of preservation. At least three neighborhoods of the ancient town have been excavated, and a visitor should not miss walking through at least one of them, the neighborhood of the theater, which is very near the harbor and very well kept.

That visit ought to give a very good idea of what the ancient city felt like, as one can visit houses, shops, and streets, thus acquiring a good initiation into the spirit of everyday life in ancient times.

The Work of Archeologists

Living in and handling archaeological material is a particular state of mind. The purpose is to eventually "read" it. Until one arrives at that point, however, the point when the stones speak, a certain

Excavation of Temple of Aphrodite, Delos Greece by the French School Archaeologists and students.

handling of this material is necessary to let the stones express themselves. That is, one has to be particularly careful in handling it and respect the fact that the item must get to live longer. One has to consider that it was the rubble that cocooned it for thousands of years, and now we are exposing it to further deterioration after the excavation. All these respectful considerations give us time to look and note the material, become conscious of its existence, and start thinking the "what is it game" from which we shall get our common sense answers always considering the hows and the whens. There is a whole array of archaeologists who specialize in every aspect of life in the ancient times. We have people who collect and study thousands of broken pottery shards with the purpose of restoring them and studying ancient life further on. I mention broken glass specialists, broken roof tile collectors, dissolved mosaic pieces collectors, even wall plaster collectors who are reconstructing the original frescoes, and the list goes on. All these people are dedicating their lives to putting together the most interesting puzzle of them all: our past and our history. It is the learning from the experiences of this history that will help us go into the future with at least a confident posture.

Precautions for Your Visit

At this point, I would like to caution you that like in every museum the place is guarded and it is prohibited to do any more damage to the ruins. One may not climb onto walls or marbles or take any "souvenirs." Also, it is advisable always to walk on the beaten paths that are clearly visible. Trekking on the rubble mounds or walking in terrain covered with grasses where there might be excavation pits or hidden irregular flooring, is not a good idea. At any cost you should avoid accidental injuries since there are no medical services on the island. Comfortable, flat, non-sandal shoes are recommended for this site.

Map of the Archaeological Space of Delos

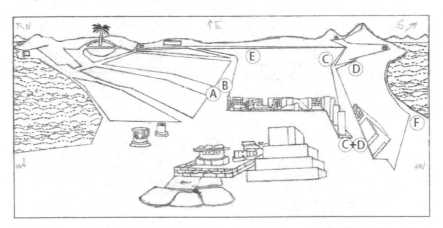

Entry Point to Delos:Main Port Square or Ancient Market Place of the Competaliasts

Six main paths are shown, A,B,C,D,E, F. They eventually interconnect except in the case of coastal path F.
A. Path of the sacred way through the temples of Apollo and Artemis and onto the statues of the Lions and the Sacred Lake.
B. Path to the museum and coffee house
C. Path to the Temple of Aphrodite, House of Hermes, and the Temple of Isis. (This path is best taken after Path D unless there is a specific need to go there first)

D. Path to the neighborhood of the theatre and on to Mount Cyn thus.

E. Path from the museum to the Temples of Isis and Hera and the top of Mount Cynthus.

F. Coastal path to the Temple of Asclepius and ancient hospital.

This square was an open air market by the port, a commercial area. All around the square, the single rooms were shops. Holes on the pavement here and there were for the wooden poles supporting the tents of the open-air stalls, just like those in a bazaar. In the center of the square there are the remnants in marble of monumental shrines dedicated to the gods of commerce.

In this market square feasts were celebrated during which there were offered to the gods fruits, incense, and roasted piglets. They were religious rituals, and the whole island celebrated. It was a day for merriment with a lot of spectacles going on, like wrestlers competing for an amphora (a large Greek jar or Grecian urn) of wine, or the hams of the sacrificial piglets.

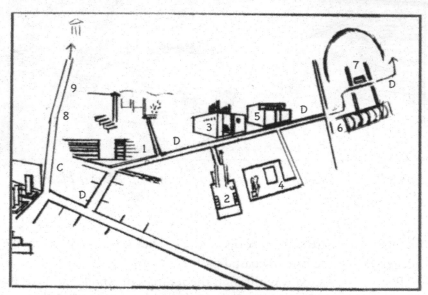

Map for Paths C and D. Path C - to the Temple of Aphrodite (8) and the House of Hermes (9) and on to the Temple of Isis — Path D - to the excavation of the neighborhood of the theater and on beyond to the hotel, the House of Masks, and the House of the Dolphins up to the mountain region. Eventual connection with path E

Path C - To the Temple of Aphrodite and the House of Hermes and on to the Temple of Isis

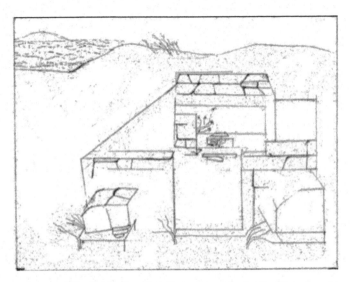

Remnants of the Temple of Aphrodite - Path C, Number 8

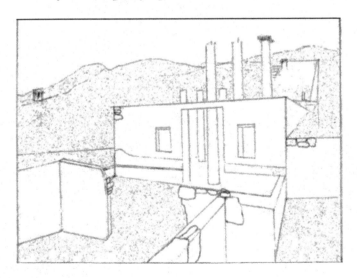

House of Hermes - Path C, Number 9 - to the excavation of the neighborhood of the theater and on beyond to the hotel, the House of Masks and the House of the Dolphins and to the mountain region. Eventual connection with path E

Continuing up the Street from Port and Market -
Path D Number 1

In this chapter, we let you see out of the eyes of the people who lived in Delos. You will walk in their footsteps, walk into their homes, shops, and let your feet move as they did in ancient times. In your imagination, see the houses, shops, and streets become complete, alive, full of people, flowers, and statues. See the shops full with produce, with fish, perfumes, clothing. Close your eyes for a moment and see the marble stones re-assembled back into exquisite marble structures, see the city full with life and be there.

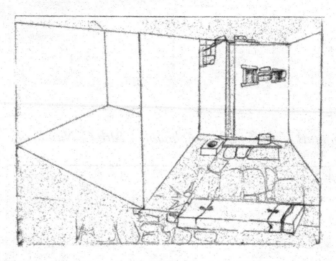

This is a drawing of one of the shops in the Theater street.

What you see in this chapter are the remnants, still very well preserved, of a neighborhood where people lived and shopped in an ancient Greek city. This part of the excavation contrasts with the excavation of the sacred area and of the temples which we discuss later on. This chapter gives you a wonderful tour of the neighborhood of the theater, a place with people's houses, and shops, and lets you immerse yourself in the life of the people in ancient times. In general, the neighborhood of the theater that we see here, from what has been found, was one of the richest and best situated, apparently an upper middle class society. It is impossible to date exactly the whole excavated section, since this was a breathing community and each single construction was used by many generations and was re-modeled each time according to the whims and needs of the people living in it. We can safely say, however, that the most of the constructions of this part of the city at least, were built within the last three centuries before Christ. Single rooms that you see everywhere are shops and workshops. It was upstairs, usually, that people lived. The walls were plastered with mortar, inside and outside, generally painted in pale pastel colors. The pavement of the street with the flagstones is the original one. At times, some modern cement was used at the time of exposure to stabilize the flagstones and the top of the walls. Under the pavement there is always a sewer, part of the main sewage system of the city that ran by gravity into the sea.

This is one of the larger, wider streets. They were all very narrow; however, because of the limited space on the island, the space between neighbors was not ample. People were living much closer to each other in those societies, in body and in spirit. From this observation, we can even deduce one of the main reasons for the advancement of our culture is being social with the sense of being also political.

The city was like a labyrinth. Although city planning had been invented, no town planning was carried out here because it followed the old existing town plan that had existed in the old times. Also, this was a community of unpredictable and very rapid historical developments.

The narrowness of the streets protected the city from the heat and the wind, but it was inevitably rather dark as the houses had more than one floor. This was a bustling street full of people, the shop keepers cramming their facades with their goods. In many of the ruins you can still see remnants of the original furniture: broken marble tables, mortars, and so on. One such marble table is shown in the illustration in one of the shops. Looking closer at the table, one sees a small drainage hole on its side. Could that possibly be a small fish market or a vegetable shop? The indications of a shop's purpose (when there is no marble inscription) can be found from the construction itself and the few remaining broken artifacts. This deduction game has enabled us to identify restaurants, wine shops, dressmakers, and of course private homes.

This drawing shows the main street of the neighborhood of the theater as it advances up the hill. To the right is a shop with a marble table left in it, probably the work table of the shop owner.

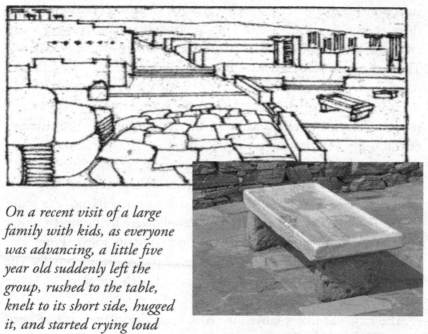

On a recent visit of a large family with kids, as everyone was advancing, a little five year old suddenly left the group, rushed to the table, knelt to its short side, hugged it, and started crying loud in joy and in tears. All stopped and watched the event astounded by the commotion the youngster was raising. His father went and tried to take him from the table but he was resisting intensely. Mine! mine! he screamed, crying and laughing at the same time. People said, "Too bad he can't take the table with him." It was as if the table was his from a previous lifetime and he now recognized it and was deeply moved. Delos does things like this. People have the deep experience of having been there before, recognizing something of a previous lifetime.

The two columns to the right, each one made from two different colored marbles, could possibly have supported a workshop for fashioning clothes. In this shop, the excavation gave us a fireplace where water was being heated in a large cauldron and six little basins of different sizes, three on either side of the room. Was this a dyer's workshop? The comparison of the setup with modern establishments probably confirms the deduction. The basins were apparently used for dyeing and rinsing the fabrics. Notice the cistern for the rainwater to supply the shop's needs.

(More on cisterns later.) On the left side of the cistern there is a small room with mosaic floor, probably the dyer's office.

House of Dionysus - Path D Number 3

This is one of the many rich private residences uncovered. All the houses (if there was enough space available) followed a basic plan: they were built around a central courtyard. This central courtyard in its turn had columns on its perimeter. The roof starts from the exterior walls and reaches the colonnade on the edge of the central courtyard, thus turning it (this central courtyard) into a large light-well in the middle of the house. All homes in ancient Greece followed this general plan. The Greeks called the central courtyard the *aethrion* (=open to the sky), and when the same mode of making houses was adopted by the Romans they called it the "atrium." Under the central courtyards of Delos there were always huge cisterns where they would store the rainwater in winter against the summer's dry season. They would pull the water out with buckets or mechanical pulleys. All the rooms are built around this atrium, having all their doors looking towards it. Windows, as we know them, were rather a rarity because transparent glass window panes had not been invented yet. Instead, they used wooden shutters for the doors and

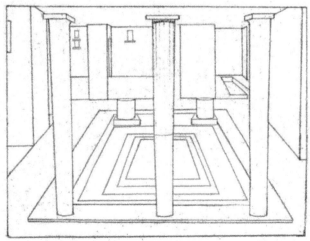

House of Dionysus central courtyard with columns around it. This courtyard or atrium is all paved with fabulous mosaics. Notice the two mouths of the cistern that is underneath. Upper right-hand side

the few windows. The usual entry and exit was a main gate and a side-door. The whole house was turned inwards, preserving its privacy, and thanks to the central courtyard there was communication

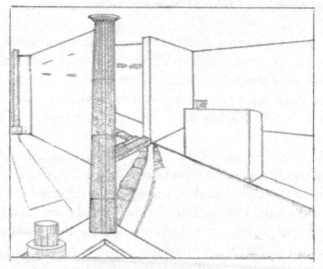

House of Dionysus reception/banquet hall. In it there is a marble base of a press to crush olives and make olive oil, and the heads of the columns (pillars) of the second floor. Niches on the walls were for oil lamps or statuettes of household gods.

House of Dionysus staircase leading to the second floor where the stone construction stops and the stairs continued in wood.

between the different parts of the house: it provided air, light, and water plus protection from heat and wind.

On top of the columns of the ground floor there was another set of columns forming the second floor. The same pattern was thus repeated upstairs: light well\courtyard, a balcony, and rooms all around. It is evident that most buildings in this area had at least one upper storey. Upstairs, usually, were the private rooms for the family: bedrooms, women's rooms, etc.; whereas, downstairs there were the general household rooms: kitchens, storage rooms, bathrooms, and always a large reception\banquet room (hall) which is easily recognizable

A house like this would be used by one single family, its servants, and its slaves.

The Mosaic Decoration of The House of Dionysus

Tiger Mosaic

The central courtyard is paved with a mosaic floor. We were very lucky that in this house one of the major pieces of mosaic art has come down to us in good condition. It represents god Dionysus with wings, in the center, riding on his favorite wild animal, a tiger. For the Greeks the religion of the god Dionysus came from the east, India. Dionysus is the god of the wine (Bacchus to the Romans). Notice the fallen wine cup and the wreath of vine leaves and grapes around the tiger's neck. He is holding the symbol of his cult, the Thyrsus (a wand or staff of giant fennel covered with ivy vines and leaves and always topped with a pine cone). Possibly this mosaic is an indication that the owner was a wealthy wine merchant (he could afford such an expensive work of art) and for that reason, a devoted follower of Dionysus. This house is now named House of Dionysus, conventionally, because of the mosaic since the name of the owner has been lost in time.

This building, which is based on older constructions, was inherited and passed through many generations. It was remodelled more than once and its purpose changed at different times. So there

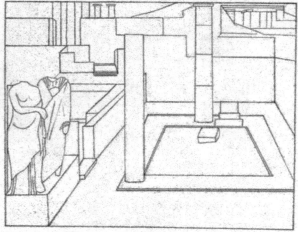

House of Cleopatra - another typical Delos house with its central courtyard and cistern underneath.

are many who call it a house, a wine serving tavern, and a brothel amongst others. The place was active through many centuries, and we cannot exclude any reasonable enterprises it may have contained.

House of Cleopatra - Path D Number 4

Notice in the center the marble altar of the household gods. The main entrance (not shown in this illustration) is facing the statues. The House of Dionysus in the background.

It is a less extravagant but wealthy home in Delos. Notice its receiving\banquet room with its simple but beautiful mosaic floor. Notice behind the statues what remains of a fountain and a place of a missing mosaic on the floor. It must have been a very fine one and thus taken away after the catastrophe. There was originally a second floor to the building as well. Very important are the two headless statues found in the house. We are even luckier to find an inscription on their base in a transliteration of Latin characters the way the ancient Greeks wrote it. On it we read: CLEOPATRADAUGHTEROFADRAS-TOSFROMMYRRRHINOUS(erected)THESTATUEOFHERHUSBAND-DIOSCOURIDESSONOFTHEODOROSFROMMYRRHINOUSFOR HAVINGOFFEREDTHETWOSILVERDELPHICTRIPODSTOTHETEM-PLEOFAPOLLONONEITHERSIDEOFTHEENTRANCEWHENTIMAR-CHOSWASARCHONINATHENS(138/137 BC)

Understanding the Inscription

We have here, obviously, a couple, who comes from a place called Myrrinous, near Athens, and who were established on Delos most likely for commercial reasons. Apparently, the family struck it rich, and the donation of the two tripods was a great event, since the tripods were big and made out of silver. The lady of the house, Cleopatra, commemorated the success of her family by erecting the two statues (the donation was widely known). This clearly was the greatest event in the family's history, as the donation is the only thing the inscription mentions. The statues were found fallen, and were replaced on their original position. The heads were never found. They date about 140 B.C.

Thanks to the inscription, we are able to confidently and accurately identify the owner of this house. In fact, inscriptions found at an archaeological dig are the only sure way of correct identification. In those days people were posting on stone a lot more than we do today. Thus we are able to find in Delos a great many inscriptions about the laws, commemorations, dedications, public accounts, and so on. By reading them we have a first-hand report of an event, and positive proof. What a difference from trying to deduce what happened from the fallen debris, which is the usual lot of the archaeologist!

The House of the Trident - Path D Number 5

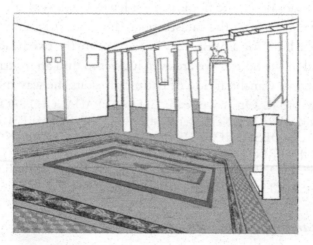

House of the Trident mosaic

The upper part of this house has been restored and on the restored roof there was definitely a second floor. The upper left door goes to the room where there was a wooden staircase leading upstairs. The mosaic floor of the central courtyard is left as found; the brilliant colors of the Greek key were obtained by using glass cubes colored with metal oxides. To the right, the marble door-like construction over the mouth of the cistern included a wheel which was used to draw water.

We know some very interesting details about this house: two half-lions and two half-bulls on the columns are the symbols of the old Syrians gods Hadad and Atagartis. (More on the Syrian gods in chapter 18.) Possibly the owner was a rich sea merchant from Syria, as we can easily infer from the two nautical themes on the mosaic floor, the anchor with a dolphin around it, and the trident (symbol of Poseidon, god of the seas). A very interesting story has been connected with this house. The oceanographer Jacques Cousteau found an ancient shipwreck on the bottom of the Mediterranean Sea outside Marseilles full of wine amphoras stamped with the symbol of the trident. It is possible that the merchant living in this house was trading wine as far away as Marseilles (which started as an ancient Greek colony about 650 B.C.).

In the middle of the reception/banquet hall under the roof, there is a hole which was the actual site of a mosaic as fine as the one in the House of Dionysus. It was, however, removed, apparently in ancient times. We do not fully understand the strange little doorless room to the left with the amphora mosaic, the trench and the hole in the floor. The amphora with its images of horse racing, also include a wreath of olive tree branches and a palm leaf which were the prizes for chariot race winners. Was this a mosaic commemorating the success of a member of the family? Was there a bench over the trench with the real amphoras—prizes of the family's winners at charioteer contests?

The partial restoration of this house and its roofing was done to protect its beautiful mosaic floors, but also allows us to see how the houses were roofed in those days. This roof is flat because there was a second floor built on it, but outer roofs were with sloping

A usual detail from Delos mosaics showing the waves of the Aegean Sea

tiles. Not all of the pieces of fallen columns were found; the new pieces complementing the old pieces can clearly be distinguished by their color. The restoration of the house starts a little over where the plaster on the walls ends. This roof, although now made of concrete, is an attempt to imitate the old style. Originally, they started with wooden beams, over which they placed planks next came an insulating layer of packed dry seaweed, then sifted deep-dug earth so that it would not contain weed seeds. Finally, they would finish the floor usually with flagstones, and even mosaics or wooden planks in certain upstairs rooms.

The plaster on the walls of this house is very well preserved. As has already been mentioned, all buildings were plastered inside and out, but it was the interior, of course, that garnered all the attention, especially in the rich houses where they were decorated with beautiful frescoes. As a general rule, the walls were covered with plaster which was molded into the shape of blocks and zones. These zones and blocks were colored with vibrant hues of red, blue, ochre, and so on. They were actually trying to pass an imitation of how the house would have looked had it been built out of blocks of colored marble or other veined stones (marble being the most elegant but also the most expensive way to build). Before the final thin layer of plaster, several rougher ones were applied. The colors from natural metal oxides were applied and absorbed while the plaster was still wet, and thus were very well preserved when uncovered. Here and there friezes were seen encircling the house with decorative themes such as flowers and Greek keys. Larger friezes would depict whole scenes from the family myths, everyday life, hunting and festivals, among other things. In this particular house a frieze with little love gods flying and playing between flowers was found. The colors, however, faded soon after exposure. The few frescoes found in the excavations which have not faded away are kept in the museum.

Mosaics

On Delos we have the largest group of ancient mosaics, about 350 pieces of all sorts from roughest to finest. The region's mosaic artists and their assistants journeyed from all around the Mediterranean to serve the wealthy of the island in this new decoration. When the Delian mosaics were made, mosaics were still a relatively new art form that was still to find its full expression of maturity.

The idea of mosaics originated when people wanted to have a steadier, water resistant, and more decorative pavement in their homes. In ancient Greece, about 500 B.C., rich people started to decorate their floors with pebbles. At first they just did designs and then as the new way of making floors developed, they began crafting figures. It was about 300 years later that the art was sufficiently developed so that they started to use small cubes chipped off marble and related stones (these cubes for mosaics are called tesserae); with this method they at last had a color variation. The great breakthrough in mosaic-making, however, was when they started to make the tesserae out of glass. They were able to color glass any way they wanted. They would tint it with natural metal oxides (rusts of metal) that are light-resistant; thus their repertoire of colors was unlimited. The mosaics we see on Delos were made at about the time that this big revolution in mosaic-making glass began.

Before a mosaic was placed, however, the pavement had to be especially prepared. A mosaic was no easy matter: the finished floor had to be able to stand weight, rain, and differences in temperature without subsiding. So, under the actual mosaic floor there are many layers of materials starting with beaten and leveled earth, followed by a thick layer of rubble, then several layers of coarse mortar (crushed bricks and lime) each finer than the preceding, until at ground level the finest of mortars would be applied on which the tesserae were actually set. Making a mosaic is an art that requires skill and speed as mortar dries fast; for that reason, they would apply the final mortar layer not all at once, but patch by patch. After the floor was finished and dried, it was polished with sand and oil. Usually before starting to put the cubes on the wet plaster they would incise the outline of the decoration theme. Rougher mosaic pieces were done on the spot (such as the mosaic around Dionysus). Very fine mosaic pieces, however, were made in the artists' studios and then applied to the floors. These were very fine works of art, made by masters who would work with tiny cubes down to 1 mm small cut in irregular shapes so that they fit perfectly, one next to another. Even the mortar below the cubes was colored to match, adding to the general effect and reducing any contrast in the joints. What they were really trying to do with these very fine pieces was to put a permanent painting on their floor. A good mosaic was greatly enjoyed and was considered fine art, like painting and sculpture. Since it was a very expensive art form, it was afforded only by the very wealthy.

A great deal of fine mosaic work decorated the upper floors as well, of course, but was destroyed with the deterioration of the buildings.

The Theater - Path D Numbers 6, 7

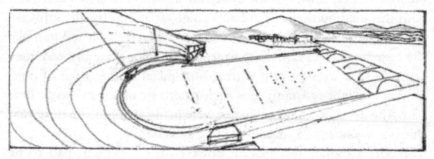

The Theater

Delos as a cosmopolitan hub was a renowned center of diversion. The god Apollo favored music, and the theater of this city had the known world's great artists visit and perform, thus pursuing prizes and recognition.

It is natural to deduce that all sorts of performances were presented. From poetry recitals to tragic plays and comedies to dances and pantomimes and especially music and songs. Every year thousands of people would participate in the festival of Dionysia, to honor the god Dionysus who was the protector of the theater arts. That festival was centered in this theater.

The festival would last four days and commenced with a big procession, beginning from the temple of Dionysus. Priests and followers with the holy symbols of the cult would ride a chariot depicting gigantic phalluses, through the main streets of the city and then enter the theater.

In honor of the gods, they would hold competitions in which young men would sing and dance hymns and present plays. At the end of the feast the winners, sponsors and artists, would be proclaimed and awarded. These hymns were esteemed highly. Between artistic events and while the theater was full, slaves would be pronounced free. The theater had a socio-religious character, and it was free of charge to anyone.

This theater was particularly busy: Delos being the island of Apollo, the god of music and arts, and considering the gay/happy personality of the Delian Apollo, this theater would host a large number of artists, actors, lyra players, cytharists, dancers, flute players, jugglers, and even marionette players. All these people would "expose" their talents to the god, and at the same time entertain the crowds.

The ancient theater in Delos

The theater was a very important social, religious, and political institution for all the ancient Greek communities. It was an indispensable place for every city: for it was here that the whole community would gather. The theater was a social miracle that created continuously more social miracles up to the present.

Even in its construction this is an exciting theater; the architects made the most of the natural formation of the terrain providing the best possible amphitheater for the actors and spectators. The lack

Public Resevoir - The cistern of the theater is one of the public water reservoirs of Delos dug and built behind the stage. Rainwater was collected here from the marble-inlaid open air theater. The arches were supporting the roof which was made of stone slabs. There were eight cylindrical marble mouths in a row from which people were drawing water with buckets.

of space at the top of the theater was solved by cutting directly into the hill and allowing the upper tiers to form an oval shape. In order to help the spectators sitting on the upper outer corners, they made the front walls not a straight line but inclined towards the center, thus enhancing a three-dimensional view of the stage rather than the two-dimensional one as it would have been had the walls been constructed on a horizontal line.

These things required extremely accurate calculations and precise building. We do not know the origins of the architects, although we have found inscriptions informing us that the public expenses for the construction of the theater lasted ten years. It is constructed on a vein of marble and made from that marble.

The theater was also the place where the inhabitants of the island would politically meet and elect their officials and decide their common fate. The democratic governance of Delos must have been admirable since Aristotle the famous philosopher visited the place, observed its proceedings and wrote a book called "The Constitution of the Delians" in which he was presenting the political system of the island to the other Greeks to imitate.

A Story: He Recreated His Voice (the Rebirth Song)

One day a tenor from a famous Opera company in New York came to Delos. He went to the magnificent theater, with its rows of marble seats in an amphitheater pattern, and then his eyes lit up and he almost trembled. He was to be starring for the first time in an opera and was afraid of this role and uncertain of his capability. Operas can be very difficult and the parts are often very challenging to singers. He came to Delos as a curious tourist and visited the ancient theater. He realized that it was one of the greatest sites in the world for sound performances albeit silent for thousands of years. All of a sudden in the silence a lark started singing (there are plenty of larks in Delos). Startled, he became conscious of the bird and his mate chirping to each other. He was aware now he had come to find the courage for his difficult career.

Later on in his visit he went to the birthplace of the God Apollo and Goddess Artemis, to the palm tree in the center of the sacred lake. Here in privacy with only the ancient Gods and Goddesses listening, he tried out some low volume singing. He raised his arms and sang an aria. As he opened up and sang, he got larger and larger and had more and more vitality and strength. His voice boomed out, full, vigorous, confidant, and alive, and it filled the bowl of the lake. He heard himself deeply, he saw his good and bad qualities and he bundled up his voice situation in confidence.

Immediately afterwards he ran back to the theater, he imagined and felt it full, with all its 6000 spectator seats. And this time he performed, for real, and the whole island heard his wonderful resounding voice until people started going to the origin of the sound, to the theater. Lucky were the few who made it on time to hear his birth song.

Afterwards, he realized that Apollo the god of music had indeed come to him and given him the ability to reinvent himself and to go on with his career and his role in this pivotal time.

The Path Up from the Right Side of the Theater Takes the Direction of the Mountain

After the visit to the "old part" of the city near the port, we shall now see the "new parts" of the city that were built during its commercial boom when many foreign people lived here. The great building in front with the restored marble gate is one of the hotels of the island, and its cistern in the central courtyard is the deepest found so far. The rows of guest rooms in corridors around the central atrium and the existence of more floors (there are the remnants of staircases) are indicative of the number of people staying there and guest lodgings required.

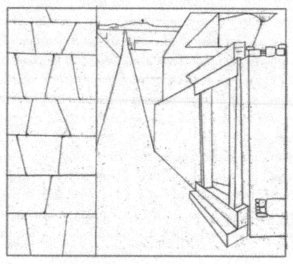

The Hotel. Continuing on the path towards the mountain we see the monumental entrance to the hotel. Advancing up the path we shall see the House of the Masks to the right and the House of the Dolphins to the left.

Above the hotel we shall visit two more exquisite houses: the House of the Masks (far right) and the House of the Dolphins (left).

In Delos there was an immense influx, all year round, of all sorts of people—pilgrims, merchants, idlers, and beggars. The temples had houses that were rented to pilgrims to offer seasonal accommodation and there were surely private homes that would also provide lodgings for a fee.

To date archaeologists have found only one building which is believed to be a hotel, a large and rather luxurious one. No doubt there were other hotels, but they are either not excavated or unidentified as yet. The hotel was several stories tall with many small rooms and rather extensive facilities. The immensity of the cistern in its central courtyard is an indication that the building was for public use. It is lined with a special hydraulic humidity-resistant, very strong plaster made out of finely crushed pottery shards, sand, lime, pumice stone and dust from the nearby volcano of the island of Thira (Santorini). In fact, all the cisterns were lined with this mix; that is why a great many of them still hold water.

Staying in a hotel for an ancient Greek was not, however, a very pleasant experience, as hotels were considered ill-famed innovations. When the ancient Greeks travelled they usually stayed with friends. This had developed into a formidably intricate system; families in several parts of the country would be bound together with old ties of mutual hospitality going back generations. Hospitality was a religious act under the protection of Zeus.

Other public accommodations were, so far as we can see, limited. Two restaurants have been uncovered, and several public baths and latrines. It is certain that there must have been many houses of pleasure operating under the protection of Aphrodite, goddess of love.

But visiting Delos was exciting in those days. There was always something going on: religious festivals celebrated with songs and dance late into the night, processions, sacrifices in which everyone could participate and share the food common to gods and men, presentation in the theater, athletic games in the stadium, horse and chariot races in the Hippodrome, pompous visits of the official embassies of different cities to offer the god their annual gifts.

Delos was indeed a place for song and dance. Apollo, its protector and the god of music and light, together with the island's commercial prosperity, made this possible.

House of the Masks

This house is partially restored in order to protect the very fine mosaics on its floors. (Most of them related to the theater: Dionysus,

The central courtyard of the House of the Masks

comedy masks, a dance.) Notice that around the rooms there was always a roofed gallery. The black stone is the house altar. Where the floor was unpaved they would cover it with a mixture of deep-dug earth and semi-burned charcoal (charred), thus insulating it from temperature and humidity and keeping the house warm. This house did not have a cistern under the central courtyard. Its cistern was the pool dug into the rock next to it. Rainwater was collected in that open-air cistern. The columns were not made out of marble, but from cheaper stone material and then plastered with white cement. A guild of actors or people working at spectacles possibly lived here. Or a wealthy man who sponsored cultural events and for that he was honored by the city. The mosaics' themes indicate such honors and activities.

House of the Dolphins

To the right is the main entrance of the house. The entrance hall is mosaic-paved; the Phoenicians' symbol of life, the tanit, was placed there as a protective symbol to chase evil spirits away and identify the owner's family roots. Symbols of a similar nature are scratched on the walls of many houses in Delos. The kitchens of the house were probably located to the left of the entrance hall; it is difficult to be sure, however, since they did not have permanent installations, but used instead portable braziers, grills, and other movable items.

There are wonderful mosaic decorations in the central courtyard: a grand rosette with many friezes, and in every corner a pair of harnessed dolphins ridden by an Eros god (Cupid). A rare case of a signed mosaic: the artist was Asklepiades from Arados.

The presence of the tanit symbol suggests that this house was owned by a merchant from Phoenicia.

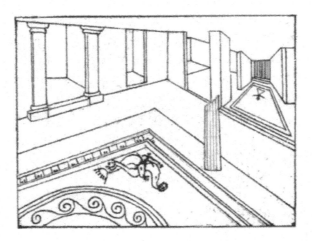

The central courtyard of the House of the Dolphins

Mosaic decoration from the House of Dolphins

Your First Glimpse of the Isle of Rhenia

You are high up on the hill now and you can see across to the island on the other side. Right across the channel on the other shore there is the island of Rhenia. It is there that the cemeteries of the community have been dug up, because there existed on the island of Delos an old religious law decreeing that no one should ever be allowed to be born or die on the island proper since this was the island where god Apollo was born and who hated death. All women ready to have a baby and everyone ready to die were transported across. There was also a law banning dogs from the island for being impure. Of the two little islands in the channel, as you are looking towards Rhenia, the one to the right is the island of Hecate (goddess of the deep night and witchcraft) and the larger one to your left is the island of Iris (goddess of the rainbow and its colors).

This overview includes practically all that you will visit in the second part of the book. This visit will take you through the sanctuary of Apollo, the Market Places and in general the downtown of the community.

SECTION THREE:

Delos as a Spiritual Space,
The Twelve Awarenesses and
The Twelve Monuments to Make Your Miracle

Chapter Eight
An Introduction for the Very Special Spiritual Visit to the Sanctuary of Delos and the Temples of Its Gods.

Our Method for Miracles and Life Change

This is a special book in which Delos becomes a place to change your life. This is an alternate view of Delos and Greek archeology. From a very old story, we have created a new method. We have taken one of the most ancient powerful healing places on earth and made a way of healing that is original, new, and ancient at once. The energy and the sacred temples are real, the history and mythology are real, and the downloads have been and are real. Delos offers this to you as a gift to heal your life and make miracles now.

We have chosen twelve energy awarenesses and twelve monuments for making miracles. On Delos, there are innumerable awarenesses and just as many excavated ancient monuments that bring them forth. We chose these twelve awarenesses, and twelve monuments where you can have the experience of a miracle, become your own oracle, and change your life.

How to Use Delos to Create a Miracle and Heal Your Life

1. There are twelve awarenesses and twelve matching monuments. From these awarenesses, at least one will call you. Read over the awarenesses and see which one resonates with you and what is happening in your life story right now. We anticipate that you will identify it.

2. Go to the monument matched to the awareness you identified with and feel it. Feel your own story, and see how this place will heal you.

3. Sit quietly in the place for some time, notice and meditate on what you have there and what you are. It may help for you to read the list of words pertaining to the place. Each word is a journey deeper into the energy of this monument and of your self.

4. You can do ceremony too, if you choose. You can give an offering, make a prayer, follow a guided imagery, make a pilgrimage walk—like a walking meditation, read aloud to yourself an ancient hymn sometimes provided, or even do further research on its particular history.

Our Twelve Awarenesses or States of Consciousness

We have chosen twelve awarenesses that were important in ancient times. Each awareness is an energy that evokes a state of consciousness that is important to making a miracle and a life change.

The twelve awarenesses are these:
1. Consciousness
2. Power and Grace
3. Oracular Power
4. Creation
5. Fertility
6. The Source of Life
7. Metamorphosis
8. Love
9. Protection
10. Victory
11. Health
12. Strength

The Corresponding Most Important Places on Delos for Miracle Evocation:

1. The area of the three temples of Apollo and his "Altar of the Horns"
2. The Temples of Artemis
3. The House of Hexagons
4. The Sacred Lake and Lions
5. The Two Graves of Hyperborean Maidens
6. The Minoan Spring or Spring of the Nymphs
7. The Temple of Dionysus
8. The Temple of Aphrodite and The House of Hermes
9. The Temple of Hera and the Temple of Isis
10. The Temple of Zeus on top of the Mountain, the Cave of Hercules, and Temple of the Good Luck Goddess
11. The Temple of Asclepius, the Hospital
12. The neighboring isle of Rhenia and its extensive cemeteries

When We Put the Awareness with the Monument That Represents It, We Get Our Method of Mystical Healing:

1. The Power of Consciousness is in the Temples of Apollo
2. Power and grace is in the Temple of Artemis
3. Oracular power is in the Monument of the Hexagons
4. Creation is in the Sacred Lake and Terrace of the Lions
5. Fertility is in the graves of Hyperborean Maidens
6. The Source of Life is in the Minoan Spring
7. Metamorphosis is in the Temple of Dionysus
8. Love is in the Temple of Aphrodite and the House of Hermes
9. Protection is in the Temples of Hera and Isis
10. Victory is in the Mountain, the Cave of Hercules and the Temple of the Good Luck Goddess
11. Health is in the Temple of Asclepius, the god of healing
12. Strength is in Rhenia—the gateway to the underworld and the passage to this one

The Idea Behind This List Is That Delos is "the Happy Island, the Island of Miracles."

So, conscious words like Oracular Power and Fertility, that "make you happy" are in essence the medicines of the Delos cures. The words are like mantras themselves; when you repeat them, hear them and see them, it is part of the ancient healing of Delos.

The structure of this part of the book is based on twelve experiences of consciousness expansion in Delos. Each experience is an awareness of its own, we take you to a stage on which a lot of things happened—healings, appreciations, assessments of experience. Delos is a place where your consciousness is rectified. It's the place for consciousness. Delos could be (is obviously) one of the consciousness organs of the living-planet earth.

We give you twelve examples to use for anything in your life that needs healing. Unhappy consciousness is the problem, that begins the flow of healing, it is the starting point. Illness is a consciousness problem, healing is rectifying consciousness. It is the most ancient foundation of body, mind, and spirit medicine—sometimes called "psychosomatic" in modern terms.

The integrity of the monuments was seriously damaged during the abandonment years so the remaining ruins are only a meager reminder of their original stature. Time takes a lot away, therefore spiritual archeology has to make up for the missing parts. In ancient times, people brought their consciousness to make up the missing part, and now, you need to make up for the missing part by being conscious of your life story which is what you possess. The point of your visit is to appreciate where you are and to proceed to your self-transformation.

Each of the following chapters has two parts. The first is academic, with the archeology, the evidence of what was excavated, and what was found and conclusions deduced. The second is its corresponding symbol and its pertaining words. First we talk about the ancient story, the myth. This will orient you to the site, where it is, how to find it, and what it was in ancient times according to the excavations. Then we have instructions for what to do there. In each site, what you do comes from what is there for you, a stone or a wall or a fragment. One place may have a bench, another a cave, another a mountain top. Your perceptions and feelings will come from the ancient energies and resonance of each place. We also have the stories of what happened to other people in the same place. When you read the story, remember, it is about what happened to that man, that woman. You will think, how does it apply to me? and you will then make your own story. One that is yours and is about your life. It will be like this.... You will have read the book.... You will then decide to go to one place. At the end, you will have had a concise experience where you feel the particular energy and do something to heal. That is how this will be a guidebook for spiritual archeology, a guide to moving about and being conscious and self-aware.

Our Magic Words

Each awareness and place has its own magic words pertaining to it. These words appear at the end of each chapter like mantras or spells. They will be your guide to the ceremony in the place that calls to you and that which you chose, the one that resonates within your body. Each word is a mantra to help you identify with its energy and embody it, consciously. The words are the tools of every chapter, the hardware of the medicinal parts of the book. When you say the words to yourself, at a monument, you are transformed.

For example, Health has the words:

- **Natural Vigor** - which is stimulated by the energy of the land around the hospital
- *Aroma* - aromatic oils, flowers, the sea, food
- **Ambrosial sensations** - the smell of nature around you
- **Floral Essence** - prepared from flowers to heal body mind and spirit
- **Exuberance** - a feeling of well being of body, mind, and spirit
- **Blooming Fullness** - how you feel after being healed
- **Safe and Sound** - the feeling of security
- **Elixir** - have a sip of water
- **Heyday** - a fantastic day, the peak, the best day of your life

At the end of each Chapter, we define each magic word so you can go deeper into the consciousness of Delos. When you do your ceremony at the site, and do your guided imagery, you can picture, imagine, and say the words. For example, at the hospital with health, you can say vigor vigor over and over again as you stand on the altar of Aesclepius there.

We Have Chosen from the Decorations On Ancient Ceremonial Ceramics Twelve Symbols Used to Evoke the Awarenesses

From its very beginnings, Delos spoke in emotions, then in symbols, then in monuments. We celebrate this here, in this book. The whole island is a symbol of transformation of consciousness, of expansion of consciousness. This is what makes you your own oracle and creates the miracles.

That is why we also found twelve emblematic symbols in the excavations on broken ceramic shards that stood for the awarenesses even before the written word came about. These ancient symbols were used as life-changing and/or spiritual communication. We pair each symbol with an awareness and with a corresponding monument, that way each symbol and each place will resonate with the myth behind the site and with your own personal story. The word "aesthetics" comes from the Greek verb feel, feelings, and this is what we will do with the symbol shapes. The symbols at the beginning of each chapter will help you to map out your personal healing journey to Delos beyond the level of words.

The Symbols That Will Start Each Chapter and are Used in Footers are These:

1. Power of Consciousness

2. Power and Grace

3. Oracular Power

4. Creation

5. Fertility

6. The Source of Life

7. Metamorphosis

8. Love

9. Protection

10. Victory

11. Health

12. Strength

Your Own Healing Path to a Miracle

The twelve monuments can be visited one at a time as a sacred life changing pilgrimage. When you do this, each builds on the energy and consciousness of the one before, and you grow towards your miracle. Or, you can choose which particular sites interest you and visit them one after another. Or you can pick one site and stay there for your whole visit. Any way you do it, your visit is a sacred path of awareness.

When you visit the twelve sites in order, it turns into an intentional path to change your consciousness and create a miracle. The first nine places are very close to each other and can be visited in a circle. The climb of the mountain is further, and the hospital and Rhenia can only be seen with a guide privately or done as a meditation. So... here you go.

Your Twelve Visit Path to Create a Miracle:

1. Start at the Temple of Apollo. Here is the birth of your journey to expand your consciousness. Apollo hates death and begins your journey to rebirth. This visit is the beginning of your journey to your new consciousness and your own miracle. It is also the healing of the divine masculine within you.

2. Next go to the Temple of Artemis to visit grace and power. Here is the center of female energy, on Delos, equal here to the male energy. (Remember, they were twins.) Artemis is strong enough to appease death and be conscious of it while at the same time, creating all with birth. The female gives birth to life and to death. Find and heal your divine feminine here.

3. After you are awake, conscious, and have realized the divine masculine and divine feminine, you go to the House of the Hexagons to become your own oracle. Oracular power is about the future. Once you have consciousness of your present and the marriage of male and female in you, you are ready to look ahead and see the future.

4. Then you are ready for creation of your new life, so you go to the Sacred Lake and lions. Creation is the beginning of your new world. The lake was the birthplace of the two gods, and the first steps to your new life. Reorder your DNA here for your new body.

5. Then on to the Hyperborean maidens, helpers of fertility to make things grow. Fertility is the place of recreating your culture. Fertility helps you give birth. You need helpers (the Hyperborean maidens) and goddess of childbirth for an easy birth.

6. You go next to the Minoan fountain for water. The source of life is water, water feeds the seed, waters your culture, purifies, connects you to rebirth, youth, and pure intention.

7. After you are purified you can grow. To grow, you metamorphose, so you visit the temple of Dionysus. All your aspects are transformations as you grow into your true self. As you grow, you become aware of yourself in your different aspects.

8. And then move on to Aphrodite to Love. Love is the most important force. Your identity is formed by what you love. When you have metamorphosed into your sexual self, authentic and true, and have found your Spirit Lover, you make love in the temple of Aphrodite, goddess of Love.

9. Now, you start to climb, to the temple of Hera and Isis. You visit other aspects of the divine feminine—the wife, the protectress, the strong companion. You protect what you love while you are living it.

10. Finally, climb up the mountain to Victory. You have grown up, you are there, you did well—now celebrate. From the top of the mountain, you have a 360-degree, fabulous view of the world. It's time you decide your direction since the spirit manifests through its action in the world.

11. All this is healing, so you can finish your healing at the hospital, Temple of Asclepius. Here you heal, become your own healer, keep up your health, and make final decisions about your life and death

12. The conclusion is birth, death, and your rebirth into your new dimension in Rhenia. You see the portal to rebirth, and your rebirth to new consciousness and awareness is your miracle in Delos.

Every part of the island merges with your consciousness and is a part of your contemporary life. You become aware of the twelve stages at the end. The island is taking you, you follow the path and realize—this is your life. It is Delos's life, as good as any great ancient Temple, a place you go to realize yourself in the present.

Reclaiming the Divine Feminine in Delos

Delos is a wonderful place to embrace the divine feminine, the mother in us all, creator, nurturer, lover, giver, and receiver. She is the embodiment of holding and embracing. She is the container for the growth of life. She is the womb of spaciousness from which forms are created from our dreams, holding and nourishing them until they are ready to be born. The divine feminine also holds aspects of the irrational, nonlinear, emotional, and the vulnerable.

Delos has temples and monuments for reclaiming all the aspects of the divine feminine. The Temple of Artemis is the site to reclaim wildness, nature, dreams, freedom. The Temple of Hera is the site to reclaim the mother, creator, womb. The Temple of Aphrodite is the place to reclaim the lover, giver, receiver, embracing, nonlinear. The Minoan fountain is the place to reclaim the giver, growth, vulnerability. The graves of the Hyperborean maidens are the place to reclaim the nonlinear, mystical, giver, dreams. The Temple of Dionysus is the place to reclaim the Maenad, the wild woman, free, passionate, unbound, orgiastic.

At each temple or monument you can merge with divine feminine. At each site, there is an opportunity to merge with the part of yourself that is nurturing, generous, life giving, and receptive. The feminine is an aspect of humanity which has been long suppressed and disempowered. When we pilgrimage to Delos, we tap into the reemergence of the divine feminine.

Because, in ancient times, it was different. Some of the first healing and transformative art is about the divine feminine. Neolithic sculptures that were used in ceremony in Europe showed a large woman with big breasts and a big belly. Petroglyphs all over the earth showed the divine feminine woman in ceremony.

The Cycladic Greek sculpture showed women as if in ceremony. Ancient sites in Greece always started with the divine feminine worship, and the first statues were women with arms upraised. The divine feminine was worshipped in caves and springs, and you can find the cave and spring if you look for them in most Greek archaeological sites. In ancient Greece the oracle was a divine feminine woman. In Delphi, she sat on a tripod chair with a hole for vapors under her where the oracle was read. In Delos it was the same, the first temple was to Artemis, the temples to Hera are near a spring so water can be used for purification ceremony. In Delos, there are also divine feminine sites that portray the dark unknown feminine. This aspect of the divine feminine has always been celebrated in ancient religions. In Delos, Artemis is the goddess of birth but also death. She takes women in childbirth away. She is the goddess of sacrificial ceremony and has this aspect to her worship, too.

To be open and creative, you need to allow what is irrational to be expressed so it can be seen, heard, and embraced. The divine feminine does not need to make sense. You don't have to understand or explain who she is for you. She does not have to make sense and can be irrational. To discover this aspect of the divine feminine in Delos, go to the Temple of Artemis. See her as the wild nature goddess, go the Temple of Aphrodite and see her as the passionate lover, go the Temple of Dionysus and see the Maenads running naked chasing the god. Give yourself permission, you don't have to understand or figure it out. Just be with it. One of the reasons we talk about the divine feminine is that our Western culture has been dominated by the masculine. Science, technology, linear thinking and other aspects of the masculine dominate our society, our institutions, and our humanity. The reason we are addressing the radiance of the divine feminine is about returning the aspect of ourselves that is creative, erratic, irrational, emotional, caring, and nurturing. Delos helps us see that the divine feminine was crucial to balance and harmony. Many of our twelve places for miracles are feminine and are, in fact, about reclaiming your divine feminine.

When you do ceremony in Delos to make a miracle, you bring the divine feminine back into your body and bring this way of caring back to your life. This is an important part of how Art as a Healing Force heals you and people you love around you. The divine feminine is a necessary part of caring, of loving, and of any healing. The Chinese medicine way of looking at this in medicine is that yin energy is nurturing, healing energy and yang energy is action-oriented healing energy. Modern western medicine has put yin energy to sleep. Science has taken over, and caring, loving, nurturing have been displaced by technology.

Marrying the Divine Masculine with the Divine Feminine

In addition to having lost a connection to the divine feminine in our culture, the divine masculine is also a concept we have lost. In our culture masculine is often portrayed as violent, materialistic, domineering, and destructive. In ancient times the divine masculine was completely different. Delos highlights this more inclusive and complete view. Apollo, the Greek god of the sun, was the god of music, oracular power, consciousness, medicine, and light. You can see the divine masculine was much different than the masculine image modern feminists talk about. The divine masculine is about penetration, seed, energy, light, creation, trance, healing, and inner travel. In Delos, you can connect with the broader, more complete divine masculine. If you visit the Temple of Apollo, you connect with the divine masculine as the god of consciousness, medicine, and oracular power. The Temple of Dionysus allows you to connect with the divine masculine as trance, visionary state, sex, death, and rebirth.

In Delos, there is also an opportunity to reunite the divine feminine and divine masculine within ourselves and create an experience of wholeness and personal integration.

Many cultures had a sacred marriage of divine feminine and divine masculine as an important basis of ceremony. Many clay sculptures showed the mating of the divine feminine and divine masculine. The *Hieros Gamos*, or sacred marriage, was important in Sumer, Egypt, and ancient Greece. The island of Delos in Greece was the birthplace of the twins, Artemis Goddess of the moon and Apollo God of the sun, and was about merging these two energies. The bee priestesses or Melissas led ceremony in ancient Greece with the union of divine feminine and divine masculine. Followers of Dionysus had sexual ceremony to celebrate the union of energy. Tantra in India and Tibet has ceremony for the union of divine feminine and divine masculine to achieve enlightenment. These art and healing images, paintings, sculptures, dances, and ceremonies are deeply healing by bringing the opposites together and merging them as one. In Delos, they were celebrated by lovemaking in ceremonies of Dionysus, where the divine feminine and divine masculine were worshipped in their mating.

When you do ceremony to reclaim the divine feminine and divine masculine, you resonate your consciousness as one whole. Part of the process is that both aspects inside you fall in love with each other. This is a manifestation of the ancient Spirit Lovers of the sacred marriage, the first lovers in human history, myth, and legend that represented the birth of all things. They are inside everyone. When they are seen and recognized, they bring wholeness to our soul.

In Delos, the divine feminine seduced the pilgrim to dance with her, and a magical integration takes place. The divine feminine and divine masculine merge, and a magical collaboration takes place that is nothing less than spiritual and healing. This was an important part of the miracle that Delos made for thousands of years and still makes today.

The Essence of This Book

The essence of this book is our personal interpretation of what Delos does to people. We make this interpretation by looking deeply at what Delos does to us. This is a book about our personal experience of miracles and life change in Delos. The general guideline of the book is that Delos gives you an outlet or an open window, where a shift happens. This has huge repercussions on your affairs, and that is what you have to integrate.

Delos speaks: first pay attention. Be here now. Let all your worries and concerns disappear. Open your eyes. Feel yourself. Look around you…. That is a shift into sacred space, Delos is calling you home.

The miracle happens from inside, from inside of you, for you. It does not come from outside you. Delos is an entrance to your own personal story. You don't need to know what is happening or why—just experience its effects on your life. That is what we did before starting this book.

How and why does Delos do this? A miracle requires a lot of your participation, you need to be active and do things to get the miracle. You need to come to Delos, to let go, to listen, listen, listen, to feel, feel, feel your own story, to know yourself. In Delos, you become center stage—a big projector is shining a light on you.

The place is so old. Delos is a story like this—growth, deeds, destruction, abandonment. It is a huge story of a huge life. It packs time into a nutshell and shows it to you with a time lag. Delos condenses time; It's a time machine, a time capsule. So, a person sees his or her whole life in a moment condensed. You see what is important, now, in the context of your own life. You are looking at everything under the sky in its whole context…and at the same time you are being shown birth and death by looking at the isle of Rhenia.

Chapter Nine
The Sacred Visits

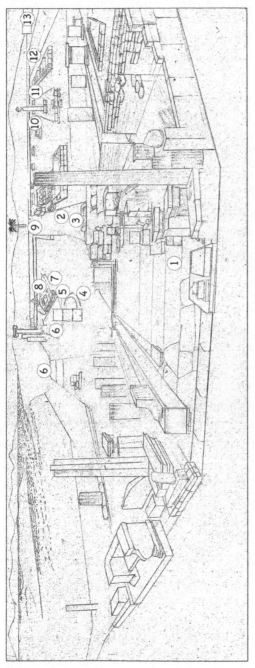

Entry to the sacred way. The main passage from the port to the sacred grounds

1. Path A - Path of the Sacred Way
2. Temples of Apollo
3. Marble base of Colossal statue of Apollo
4. Altar of the horns
5. Tomb of Hyperborean maidens 1
6. Area of Oracles
7. Temple of Artemis
8. Remnants of Apollo statue hips and torso
9. Statues of the Lions and the Sacred Lake
10. Tomb of Hyperborean maidens 2
11. Spring of nymphs or Minoan Spring
12. Phallic monuments Temple of Dionysus
13. Museum

The Sacred Way

Being the central part of the community, it was here that the most impressive and important buildings were. These were temples, porticoes, marketplaces, special buildings housing the treasures of the gods, political and administrative buildings, and other buildings of a public nature. They were made mostly out of marble, and that being always an expensive stone to quarry, it was taken away after the abandonment of Delos by the inhabitants of the neighboring islands as building materials. That is why the ruins here are not so impressively preserved as the other ones we see in the mainly residential neighborhood of the theater. However, they are more important, archaeologically, since they are the testimonials on the public way of life of the community of Delos. The poor state of preservation of the Sanctuary and its archaeological importance have turned it into a fascinating and very difficult puzzle; archaeologists by using inscriptions, scarce information given by ancient Greek authors, and a great deal of intuition have tried for a century and a half to make something out of it (delicate syllogisms, deductions).

Pilgrims would enter the sanctuary through the Sacred Way (1). Indeed this monumentally paved and lavishly decorated avenue with public benches, statues and colonnaded porticoes, was a suitable introduction to the splendor of the Sanctuary itself. It was here, on both sides of the way that a great deal of the public life of Delos was happening, and decrees honoring individuals for their virtues or declaring donations were posted. The idle visitors of Delos could spend here a good part of the day, browsing and encountering newcomers.

As for the visitors themselves, they must have been thousands. Already in a poem (7th century B.C.) performed allegedly by Homer on Delos, we see that the islanders, who were Ionians, one of the two main Greek tribes, would gather here. Their name came from Ion, their mythical ancestor, son of Apollo and an Athenian princess. The Ionians from the Aegean islands, Athens, and their cities in Asia Minor would gather here with their wives and children to honor Apollo and their common origin. This was the greatest assembly of the Ionian tribe, and it must have also had the character of a political gathering. These early islanders worshipped Apollo with songs, dances, and games. We do not have many organizational details about this feast, but what is striking is the joyfulness and the fame of the occasion.

Later on, at an unknown date Greek cities started to send to the island official religious embassies that would arrive all year round. Such embassies/delegations were formed by some of the most respected citizens who brought their cities' annual offerings to Apollo. These delegations sacrificed, offered their gifts to the God's treasuries, sang and danced. They also had the privilege to watch the performance of Apollo's Delian Maidens a very famous performing group of antiquity. These embassies came from all over the Greek world, but the most important of them was the Athenian one. They arrived with one of their sacred ships called Delias or Paralos, loaded with the gifts to the god, with dancers and singers, choral groups and musical performers to honor the god, and animals to be sacrificed. This occasion was of great importance for Athens, not only for religious reasons, but for political reasons as well, Delos being the island of the Ionian god, the Athenians wanted the god to favor them and protect their enterprises. While the sacred Athenian ship was away on its sacred mission in Delos, no criminal was allowed to be executed in Athens by law. (We learn from Plato that Socrates' death was postponed for some time for this very reason.)

There were many festivals in Delos for other deities too, but the greatest event throughout the centuries of its history was the festival of Apollo celebrated in early spring. Except for the annual festival of Apollo there was an even greater celebration every four years. During these festivals other than the animal sacrifices and festive meals, the hymns and the dances. there were athletic games in the stadium of Delos, chariot races at the hippodrome, singing, dancing, and musical contests at the theater. The prizes to the winners were tender palm branches from the sacred tree of the twin gods.

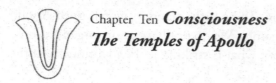

Chapter Ten **Consciousness**
The Temples of Apollo

Awareness: Power of Consciousness at the Temples of Apollo

Awareness is about having your consciousness refined, it is about a mental state. The Temples of Apollo were places of awareness, of consciousness expansion in Delos. Awareness, being aware begins with your posture. If you really want to be aware and feel the proof of being aware, your posture is the key. The way you are holding your body and awareness of your beauty is the first step in being there.

Awareness is paired with the Temples of Apollo because Apollo is the god of awareness—a gift of the power of consciousness. The area of the temples of Apollo is the strongest point of awareness and enlightenment on Delos.

Positioning Yourself on the Monument: In Front of the Temples of Apollo

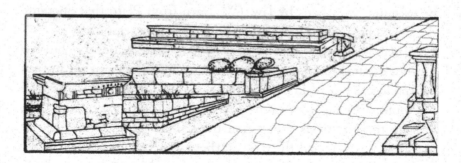

The foundations of the three temples of Apollo, the largest one is on the upper Right of the drawing, the middle one is the remnants of the Temple of the Athenians, and the one to the left is the earliest temple to the god , the one called the limestone temple. Front right, and front left there are the remnants of statue bases of famous kings, patrons of Delos.

The Temples

When you arrive at the three Temples of Apollo, stand in front of the larger one, called the Temple of the Delians, and walk around it. Look around you, at the broken pieces of marble, the columns, the large stones that constituted the temple. Look at the foundations lying on the earth. Now imagine the columns standing, white in the sun; imagine a marble colonnade all around the rectangular temple; picture the triangular top all in marble (the pediment). Imagine inside, precious statues of God Apollo, standing, looking at you.

The statue of Apollo inside was made of gold and ivory parts, formed around a wooden frame. It showed the Delian god as a young, beautiful man, wearing a belt and holding in his right palm small golden statues of the three graces standing and in his left, a bow. It was very similar in looks to the colossal statue of the god right outside.

On either side of the temple's entrance (towards the sea) there were two silver tripods, oracular vessels like cauldrons on three feet, in which charcoal was burning. The pilgrims threw incense on the charcoal, and the burning incense produced the odors that made Delos the "sweet smelling island" of the ancient writers.

A portrait of Apollo wearing a laurel wreath from an ancient vase

This area was also decorated with innumerable statues, each statue was part of the history of the god, his island and of Greece. This was education and history, people could read the inscriptions on the statue bases or even hire special people, guides, to explain the history to them, to learn history and art, do ceremony, and be taken around.

Next to the big Temple of Apollo there are the remnants of the two older temples to the God, Also behind and next to them exist the foundations of five buildings that housed the art collections of the god, offerings of the rich and pious, which were shown to the visitors, educating them about art. The remnants of these three temples, with the oldest one to the left, are the testimony of the evolution of the cult of the god of consciousness.

It was here in front of these temples that the processions would end and the pilgrims would dedicate their gifts to Apollo. The gifts would range from items of beauty, such as decorated flasks of perfume, to gold and silver crowns, to money, paintings, and statues, depending on how rich the pilgrim was and how he wanted to direct his piety and please the God. One can imagine how moving the moment was for each pilgrim who had left his home so long ago, to travel through difficult conditions, to have the god of the island bestow his grace upon him.

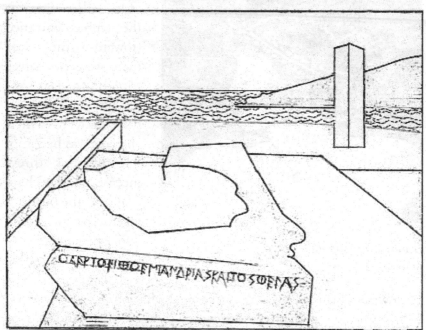

The marble base of the colossus. The old inscription on it says, "I am of the same stone the statue and the base"

More Details on the Three Temples

The oldest of the temples is on the far left. It was built in 540 B.C. out of porous stone. It was humble and small and inside there was the early statue of the god Apollo crafted by the two famous artists of deep antiquity, Tectaeus and Angelion.

This was the representation of the god that most pilgrims venerated because it was old and precious and was considered sacred art. It was very much the symbol of Delos portraying the god's most important characteristics and that being the official statue it was the pride of the Delians as an independent island community with its own traditions and culture. It was moved later once the larger temple was completed.

The temple in the middle is called the temple of the Athenians because it was built and donated to the god by the city of Athens in 425 B.C. It is by far, architecturally the most important of the three temples; it was made entirely out of marble which had been quarried in Athens. It was the same marble used in the construction of the Parthenon. From the study of its foundations we have strong reasons to suspect that the architect was Callicrates, one of the masterminds behind the construction of the Acropolis. In this temple there were seven statues dedicated to the god, standing on a semicircular bench. That is why it was called the temple of the seven statues. Statues from the outside structural decoration of this temple have been found and their fragments are shown in the museum of the island. From this magnificent gift one can easily see how important a role the Athenians played in the life of the island, and how important this island was for the Athenians themselves. By controlling such a rich religious sanctuary the Athenians harnessed the power of both money and god.

The largest of the temples to Apollo was the one to the right which was called the temple of the Delians, and it was indeed a temple built and dedicated to the god by the inhabitants of the island. The inhabitants of Delos wanted to counter the influence of Athens, and started building the temple in 478 B.C. Its construction was sporadic, depending on the politics of Delos at the time. Many parts of its columns and building blocks have been identified; however, the problem is finding the necessary funds for its reconstruction.

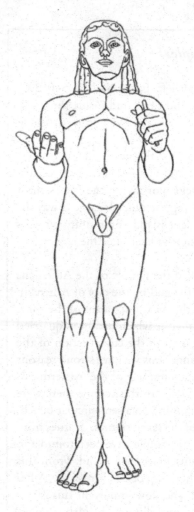

The Colossal Statue of Apollo
- artist's rendering

The two rectangular constructions on the left side of the temples are bases of statues. Especially the one on the right belongs to the grand statue of Philetairos, a great ruler who reigned from 281 to 263 B.C. in the kingdom of Pergamum, and who liked to donate great gifts to the sanctuary. He loved the fine arts and his library and museum were world famous.

The Colossus

Right in front of the entrance to the big temple there is a huge slab of marble. This was the base of a thirty foot high statue—the colossus, a huge effigy of Apollo, the god who showed each man the potential for his inner and external beauty. It was an enormous standing sculpture of a beautiful, naked young man. Apollo was the god of the culture of body and spirit. The main sculptures in Olympia were of Apollo. Apollo was the early supporter of athletics and physical fitness and beauty. He was extremely handsome and this gives us the epithet Apollon (Apollo-like) for a beautiful male. He stood there as a handsome, fit, athletic young man, a standard of male beauty inviting onlookers to be like him, handsome and graceful.

This statue which was about 10 meters tall was a gift from the city state of the island of Naxos. It dates about 600 B.C. and the inscription on its side informs the impressed viewer that the same

This very old engraving shows us Delos before it was excavated. Everything is ruined and in total disarray. It is very interesting to see the colossal statue of Apollo with it's head still on it. From the engraving until now the head has been lost into time.

stone piece was used for the statue and its base thus intensifying the amazement of the feat of "from one huge stone made into a statue." From this we understand a gigantic piece of marble (roughly resembling a statue) was brought here immersed while hanging between two rafts from Naxos 40 miles away, an island which has been famous from deep antiquity for its marbles and related industry. The piece was sculpted on Delos, here in the sanctuary, and it was up and standing as the symbol of the island for a thousand years, well even after the destruction of the city. It fell down however in a big earthquake at about 300 A.D. and it broke into pieces many of which along with other marbles were put in lime kilns for the production of masonry lime.

Two big pieces of the statue the Venetians tried to ship to Venice in the middle ages, but they could not do it because they were heavy and bulky to manage so they are left on the ruins of the temple of Artemis a few yards away.

The Myth Behind the Place: Apollo

The main god of Delos was Apollo, the god of awareness, of consciousness, of the mind and the body. He was close to his father Zeus and knew more than any other god the will of his father. Apollo was not a stereotypical patriarchal male at all. He was the god of these:

1. light
2. sun
3. consciousness
4. music
5. harmony
6. oracular power
7. medicine
8. male beauty

His famous motto from the philosophy of his cult is "know thyself." He was the god of awareness, of consciousness, of thinking clearly and seeing every situation clearly. This clarity made him the god of medicine and healing, and through him we know how to heal, respect the cosmos, and understand the music, the harmony of systems. He was the god of healing and in ancient times was the god of the healing songs sung by healers.

He had the power to heal and destroy. For those that did not follow the divine laws he could be lethal. He hated arrogance and hubris and punished trespassers with his 'toxon' (=bow); it is from this god's bow that the word toxic orininates.

The term "harmony of the spheres" comes from his kind of universal harmony. He gave shape to the formless and asked for compliance to rules. He showed how to embellish and have form, to understand how things hold together. This meant that Delos and Apollo taught people to enlarge their consciousness and adapt to their problem, to get larger and solve life's problems this way. His knowledge of the arts allowed him to be an oracle. As the god of light, he was the synonym for life: Apollo held out his hand and made visible order from the dark chaos. He is the daily light giver, riding his chariot across the sky every day. From Apollo came the healing sanctuaries of ancient Greek medicine, the oracles and dream healing, and through his son, Asclepius, came modern medicine. Also, Apollo was the god of the golden mean, of balance, with the motto "Do nothing in excess."

Apollo was not only the god of light, of the sun, of being seen… he was also the god of illumination, of feeling the light within. He was the god of the inside awareness/consciousness, defining human nature and intent for the first time.

Thus he was an inviting example with his gorgeous human form through his statue/s and because of the awareness of his light, the inside world of being human was also defined and mapped. In our western culture, words like justice, freedom, truth, and beauty amongst many others define and map the illuminated/conscious world inside a human being.

Apollo says you are a human male, you are a man with a body and you should look like me. Look at the statue of me as a 19-year old athlete, I am huge, but you must look and feel the light just like me. That is god Apollo… this illuminating data about your inside world can make you an oracle of your own life.

The Keraton: or the Altar of the Horns

In front of the temple, we have the remnants of an open space/square paved in bluish marble tiles. In the middle of this area there are the remnants of "the famous Altar of the Horns of the God Apollo in Delos." This the most important monument of the sacred island and it was the one that had to be doubled in the story of the Delian problem. In ancient times it had a canopy. This was a place where special rituals were performed, it was the place of legend. In myth, it was said that Apollo himself started it from the horns of wild goats he and his sister Artemis shot with arrows when he was four days old. They sacrificed the goats and then used the horns to create an altar, and the tradition was kept up until the last days of Delos. From animals that were sacrificed, the horns were taken and were inserted/added to an elaborate construction of interwoven serpentine braids all made of horns that made up the altar.

Around this immensely admired altar, songs, music, and dances were performed as part of the Delian ritual to the god, and all foreign pilgrim groups were outdoing each other in pleasing the god by filling his home with merriment.

The History of the Place

Through the ages, ancient writers described the Altar of the Horns as one of the wonders of the world. Every pilgrim wanted to see the Altar of Horns once in his or her lifetime, to see what Apollo and Artemis had started forming, and participate in that formation, with their sacrifices in ceremony, thus identifying themselves with their godly nature. (The multitude of horns represented Apollo's importance.) In references to the altar, found in old inscriptions, it is said that resins were bought and used to varnish the Altar of Horns and protect it from wind and rain. Later it was all protected by a canopy.

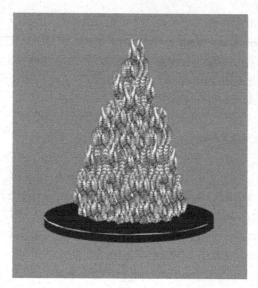

The Altar of the Horns artist's rendition

We only have scant remains of what was the building that contained the Altar of the Horns. We know it was a low walled area with an apse on one of its sides and open to the opposite. It had no permanent roof, instead it was covered by a canopy. We can safely say that because of the apse shape in the building the altar was round, most probably placed on a round base. The pilgrims were entering the building from the side opposite the apse, holding the horns of the animals that previously and possibly somewhere else had been sacrificed to the god, and going about the apse and around the altar they were stepping on the base in search of an available space in the braids of horns to piously insert their horns in turn. With all that in mind we could conclude that the shape of the altar could be something resembling a modern tree but all made of entangled and twisted braids of horns inserted one into each other.

Outside and around the enclosure of the Altar of the Horns, pilgrims performed the dance of Geranos, or the Crane dance. According to Plutarch, an ancient writer, Theseus, the mythical founder of Athens, after killing the Minotaur in the Labyrinth of Knossos in Crete, came to Delos and danced with the young Athenian men and women he had saved from the Minotaur.

This dance is connected with the labyrinth and Ariadne, who showed her lover Theseus the way out of the maze with the ingenious idea of unwinding a ball of twine. In Delos, they danced in the square around the altar of Apollo the Altar of Horns. Somehow this ritualistic performance of getting in and out of the Labyrinth marked a new awareness, and they were thankful to Apollo for that.

This dance was a special new dance with serpentine movements that imitated the movements one made to escape from the Labyrinth. It symbolizes escaping the vertigo of the labyrinth. Learning the way out of the labyrinth = enlightenment. It was taught as a dance to the young women of Delos, the Deliads or Delian Maidens, and they in turn, taught this dance to pilgrims coming to Delos thereafter. The dance was so famous that it is mentioned by Homer and by many other ancient writers. The Deliads' choral performances were so great that many ancient writers speak about them as something extraordinary. These famous singing and dancing maidens passed the ceremony and their dancing and singing art on through the generations.

After the dance, there was

This is a picture of the Minotaur from an ancient vase

*An early universal representa-
tion of a labyrinth that is to be
seen in many human cultures
including the one in Delos*

the great feast, people ate the
meals from the sacrifices, and
everyone went into wine and
merriment. This was an occasion for poor people to eat meat,
drink, dance, and sing. The
great ceremony was organized by the administration of the sanctuary and the city, and on many occasions it was a regal gift from a
king. Participating in the proceedings was the dream of every trav-
eler.

We can imagine the young, beautiful dancing women, the Deliads, leading the people following the ecstatic dance, imitating the
movements that symbolized the way out of the labyrinth, the symbol of awakening consciousness out of the darkness of prehistory
which is the course of our culture. It was said that with Apollo you
could dance and drink yourself out of unconsciousness—Apollo
sang that you were actually mimicking the way out of the labyrinth.
The labyrinth was the unconscious and Apollo was consciousness....

What to Do Here: Ceremony, the Crane Dance as a Guided Im-
agery or a Dance

You can do the Crane Dance from Delos in your imagination using
the ancient steps of the Crane Dance. You can do this as a guided
imagery or as a walking meditation; you can walk for minutes or
hours in the ancient steps. You can follow in the footsteps of the
Deliads, the maidens who led people to the Crane Dance as they
came on their sacred pilgrimage to Delos

So... start walking, imagine you are one of the ancient maidens
or young men of Delos, imagine you have been taught the Crane
Dance by Theseus, as he was returning from Crete. Put one foot in

front of the other, don't worry about how to do it because there is no right way, since no one knows exactly what sort of a dance the Crane Dance really was.

It was said the dance represented the circles that Theseus coiled and uncoiled in the Labyrinth as he found his way back to his lover and the world. There are other theories that it actually imitated the fluttering love-dance of courting cranes, and that each movement consisted of nine steps and a leap. Cranes make spectacular migrations from the Tropic of Cancer to the Arctic Circle and back twice yearly, flying in V-shaped formations with loud trumpeting at an enormous height. These were important symbols of the Hyperborean Delos cult where the messengers flew to Delos from the north on the North Wind. It is one of the first ancient maze dances, a coiling snake-like labyrinthine dance, so...your conscious walk with mindful posture on the archaeological site is good enough.

You can't do this dance on Delos, it is forbidden to do dances on the archaeological site in order to let people concentrate and not be distracting. So it is advisable to do the dance in your imagination as you stand near the Temple of Apollo. Don't be afraid, in your mind, take nine steps, follow the Deliad maidens, take nine steps, serpentine pattern, like a crane... Dance to the altar of the horns in Delos.

Actually the steps are:
Link R elbow over neighbor's L
Extend R thumb to be held, bodies close together, then
RLRLR x 4
But make any serpentine movements, any steps you wish,
in your mind's eye to see how this ancient dance was done.
Remember, remember, remember....

What to Do Here: Awareness in Posture and Beauty

Reconsider your life as a maze and realize that posture and beauty are the way out of it.

When you visit the temple of Apollo, you can't do much in that exact place. Usually there are a lot of people present. Walking or climbing on the ruined monuments is prohibited. Stay on the main path. There, in your imagination, you can dance, sing, and eat. So do your ceremony for Apollo on the main path.

Here is an original invocation to Apollo found scribbled on an ancient cere-monial ceramic. You can repeat it as many times as you like. The translation is underneath the Greek text. Say it in both languages.
Βίος Βίος, Ἀπόλλων Ἀπόλλων, Ἥλιος Ἥλιος, Κόσμος Κόσμος, Φῶς Φῶς.
Bios Bios (=Life), Apollo Apollo, Helios Helios (=Sun), Kos-mos Kosmos (=Universe), Phos Phos (=Light).

Imagine what it was like, being in touch with the god of light at the exact place of his temple. It would expand your consciousness. You get a download of knowledge, of files and folders about light, consciousness, and so on into your mind. You would experience all that would be going on in front of the temple including the singing of paeans (=song or lyric poem expressing triumph or thanksgiving by choruses of young people in contests with each other) by the god of music. You would go into the temple, throw incense into the entrance cauldrons, make sweet smoke with incense. Inside you would see the statues of Apollo, the god of awareness, and you would become con-scious of the miracle that happens to you solely by being there.

This is using your mind's eye to unlock the mystery of your life within as Delos speaks. When you arrive in Delos, you invite the light into your life. Delos is the illumination on the mystery of your own life, which will transform you and open a doorway to your con-sciousness. You can make yourself more than what you are in your own life when you receive the light at Delos.

You bring your own story, your own suffering, you come to De-los, and the marble stones of Delos reflect your own personal truth. The ruin of Delos takes you "elsewhere," it takes you from the daily reality of your own life story and suffering to the inner reality of trans-formation and spirit. You become a million times more perceptive and sensitive. You become a person who downloads ancient knowl-edge and updates your own reality.

Guided Imagery for the Temple of Apollo: Drawing in the Sun

Imagine you are in the grand Temple of Apollo on delos. It is marble, large and expansive. In this place you can draw in the energy of the sun and of light.

Face the sun. In your imagination feel the sun's energy coming.

Feel... Become aware of the feeling...

Bring the sun into your body. Feel the light of the sun filling your head like a halo. Now bring it down into your throat. Down into your heart, bring the sun's energy down into your whole body intentionally, down into your pelvis.

Now imagine your whole body illuminated, hold this energy, draw down the power of the sun until you are empowered with its light. Now take slow deep breaths in and out, using your breath, your will, your imagination to empower yourself with the elemental energy of the sun. Harness this energy, expand yourself and become a pillar of light.

When you are breathing deeply and are filled with light, you are feeling the whole ambiance that is your consciousness now.

Delos is a real physical place that opens to elsewhere, out of the familiar place you are used to, to a place you have never been before. You bring your dreams, your life story, your heart.... Delos can trigger you to go deeper and remember your desires and passions, and open your heart to see all this inside you.

Words for Consciousness at the Temple of Apollo

Intellect - Apollo was the god of consciousness, thinking, awareness

Intelligence - he had perfect intelligence

Conception - consciousness is the beginning of it all, it starts here with the creation of forms

Genius - where creative ideas come from, the fountainhead of genius

Wisdom - knowing yourself, balancing all the forces

Ideal - above material forms, archetypal, godly

Percipient - all knowing, from before the beginning of time, to after the end of time

Knowledge - holding consciousness produces knowledge

Appreciation - consciousness is love of life and seeing beauty

Judgment - perfect consciousness is perfect judgment

Intuition - comes from consciousness, when you are conscious you have golden intuition

Enlighten - abundance of light

Revelation - all moments of life are revelatory

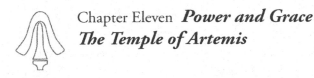

Chapter Eleven ***Power and Grace***
The Temple of Artemis

Awareness: Power and Grace, Forever Young

Feminine power is strength in action, it is the feminine force harnessed to make change. It is the force of the moon, of night light, used to heal, transform, and change your world. Feminine power makes miracles. Grace is feminine beauty in movement. It is curves, dance, is portrayed in pictures of bodies, in buildings, and in art. Grace versus money is one of the basic lessons of Delos for us today. When we lose grace, everything is lost.   Power and grace is the power of the feminine, the feminine psyche in all its beauty. Power and Grace is paired with the Temple of Artemis because this is the ancient site to restructure the feminine psyche. The Temple of Artemis holds feminine power and grace in our world.

Positioning Yourself on the Monument: The Temple of Artemis The Area of the Sanctuary of Artemis Within the Sanctuary Of Apollo

The Temple of Artemis is very old, much older than the Temple of Apollo, it is one of the oldest sites on Delos. She was there be-

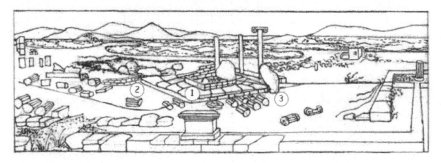

The area of the sanctuary of Artemis within the sanctuary of Apollo. 1. Temple of Artemis, 2. Tomb of Hyperborean maidens, 3. Two remaining pieces of colossal statue of Apollo torso and hips

fore her brother and it was a purely goddess site before it included Apollo. After Apollo became more important, the Temple of Artemis is within the big sanctuary of Apollo, as if she is engulfed and protected by her brother. Now, there are only the stone foundations remaining and some of the marble pieces that made up the temple. It was not large by modern standards. The scale of temples in Delos was small, but this temple is one of the larger ones.

The great surprise for archaeologists, in the Temple of Artemis as a monument, is that under the visible foundations are two other layers of foundations of older temples to Artemis. They show us how early worship to Artemis on Delos started and its development through the ages.

There three layers of temple foundations: the top one is Hellenistic (ca. 180 B.C.), the middle one is archaic (ca. 7th cent B.C.), and the bottom one Mycenaean (ca. 1400-1200 B.C.). Each foundation was a temple, each layer in time is an ancient journey into Artemis worship. Look, see, dream, each temple larger and more elaborate as the religious culture of Delos progressed. Looking into the three temples is like a time machine.

You can identify the Temple of Artemis by the presence of the torso and hips of the colossal statue of Apollo—they are next to the foundations of the Artemis Temple. There is a sign in front of it that says "Artemision" on a small stone plaque.

You can actually see the three layers of the old foundations. In one corner of the second foundation a treasure was found, artifacts of gifts to the goddess were buried in the foundations of the first temple while the second temple was being made. As each temple was remodeled, the sacred artifacts that were too old were buried in the foundations of the new temple. All the sacred offerings to Artemis were put in the earth, you can see the hole in front of the temple. These artifacts included ivory and gold statuettes and pottery belonging to early Greek culture during the time of the Trojan war, 1300 B.C. They now can be seen in the Delos museum.

The Artemision was the central power place of women in Delos. This temple was older than any other; first Delos celebrated women, before men. This temple was the place where women came to do ceremony. Inside was a statue of the goddess Artemis. The

Greeks believed that the goddess herself was inside the statue, and they fed her, dressed her, decorated her as if she were actually there. In this way, women could be blessed by Artemis and healed and transformed by her feminine power. We do not know exactly what happened in the ceremony in the Artemision, probably because it was secret and the poets who described these kinds of ceremony were men and not allowed in the ceremony. Since Artemis was the goddess of nature and wild woman, and protector of young girls and animals, maybe young women came for protection and to increase power of wildness and independence. It is possible that women came here to prepare for marriage. They would say goodbye to the wild nature life of Artemis and welcome the new life of marriage and change of status. It's up to each woman to glimpse what happened in her ceremonial visionary space.

Artemis is still there! Even without the statue, HER presence is there to heal and transform and make miracles for you now.

The Myth Behind the Place: Artemis

The first and main Goddess of Delos, Artemis, was goddess of the moon. Artemis was the daughter of Leto, the goddess of the night who generated galaxies and solar systems. Her grandmother Phoebe, Leto's mother, was a Titanide. Her great grandfather, Phoebe's father, was the sky and her great grandmother was the

This is a rendering of Artemis as " Forever Young" from a statue possibly made in Delos

Artemis from an ancient ceramic

earth, Gaia. When Leto, Artemis' mother was pregnant and looking for a place to give birth, Delos appeared to her as a ship sailing in the heavens called the Delia constellation. It was the place in the Heavens from which gods and goddesses could descend to earth.

Artemis was the embodiment of female energy, born from earth and sky. She was the female link between heaven and earth, the one who could contact and join with angels and gods. Artemis is connected to the heavens through the polar star and constellation of Ursa Major, the big bear. Artemis was worshipped in bear dances. Girls before puberty danced as bears to celebrate the incarnation of souls, or gateway to new birth. Artemis as the bear star, was identified with the winter solstice and the progression of the zodiac. She was literally star woman, moon goddess.

The realm of Artemis as goddess in human society was the protection of young girls until their adolescence, before marriage. Women of any age never abandoned her cult. They were thankful to her for life. For the protection they had received as young girls and as pregnant women, for their children and grandchildren.

The role of Artemis as protectress of young women was part of a much larger personality of the goddess as protectress of wild nature, young animal, human children or animals that were orphans at childbirth. The ancient greeks imagined and adored her as a very young woman, beautiful, extremely proud, running free in nature, enjoying the rivers, the forests, the lakes together with her huntings dogs, wild animals and nymph friends. She was young and beautiful, full of energy as nature is, always young, always renewing itself. So, her killing deers and other forest animals was a symbol of the cycles of nature: birth, growth, death.

This was Artemis for the Greeks. In older, prehistoric times (before 1200 BC) she was a lady mistress of the beasts and ald an all-purpose mother/fertility goddess. Greek mythology however, liked to give to its gods more specific realms and planes of action. So Artemis got to be the virgin of the forests; pure like the ancient forests themselves.

Artemis as goddess of the moon symbolized many energies. For

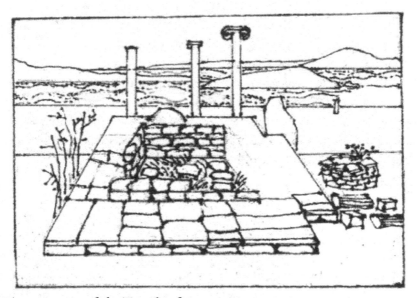

The remnants of the Temple of Artemis

ancient people, the moon stood for growth, since a woman's menstrual cycle was the same length as the moon. Artemis is always depicted young, running free, full of spring and vitality. As the holder of eternal youth, she takes care of women, children, especially orphans. She is the huntress of death and birth, she regulates life and death. Artemis helps the dead cross the straits for burial on the neighboring island of Rhenia. Artemis was the goddess of childbirth, she assisted in the birth of her twin brother Apollo on Delos. There is a special temple dedicated to Artemis for the role she plays in easy childbirth called the temple of Artemis Lochia on the hill next to the mountain in Delos that was sacred and visited by pregnant women. Women went there to pray for an easy childbirth, which was very important in that time, when many women and children died in childbirth. Artemis was also the goddess protector of the island across from Delos, Rhenia. There, she was the goddess of childbirth, and goddess of death, too. Many classical scholars consider her role as goddess of the moon key to all her other aspects, and believe it links directly with Apollo as god of the sun—brother and sister.

Artemis is described as always a virgin, since it was one of her wishes to her father Zeus when she was a little girl. There are theories that in ancient Greece, virgin meant unmarried, independent, not celibate. This would match more closely her association with childbirth, breasts (like in the statue in Ephesus), and motherhood. To some women, Artemis represents unmarried sexual activity. It is possible that the huntress had lovers, and was not bound by the need for a husband in ancient Greek life. She was wild and free and was often associated with orgiastic rites.

The History of the Place

The ancient Temple of Artemis was built before 1300 B.C. The next temple was built around it so the first would never be taken down and the religious rites could continue without interruption since they were so integral to the social life of the community. The Temple of Artemis was so sacred, so powerful it could not be closed for one day. People needed to be able to do ceremony there and adore what was inside every day. We know it was a statue of Artemis, an old wooden one from the older days of the Goddess worship which was draped with woven materials and decorated with jewelry every year, while incense was burning and flowers were offered. At the time, wealthy people who were benefited by the goddess offered precious items of silver and gold. That was the treasure of the Artemision, sacred precious items that would never get in the hands of the profane.

This fits perfectly into what the archaeological site is about, one temple inside the other, the new one built while the other was still working inside it. It allowed the daily re-virginizing to continue and was also menstrual period recurring each month, her moon. What happened inside the temple of Artemis in Delos? What ceremony was done there? This ceremony can only be seen in our imagination and felt in our bodies. Women can see it in their dreams when they do ceremony in Delos.

What did people do there? What was inside that was so important that the rites could not stop for one day? The third temple was built around the second so the rites would not stop. Women came to do ceremony in the temple of Artemis, to worship Artemis, to re-structure their feminine psyches. Each one had her own story: one would want a child, one to be woman healer, one prayed to have a regular cycle, one to be free, one to learn to cross to death, one to... who are you, what is your worship, what is your question to Artemis here?

What to Do Here: Ceremony

On two sides of this temple was a little portico where women would go and sing hymns to Artemis.

Callimachus, Hymn 3 to Artemis 170 ff (trans. Mair) (Greek poet 3rd century B.C.): "But when the maidens (nymphai) encircle thee in the dance, near the springs of Aigyptian Inopos [on the island of Delos] . . . the lights of day are lengthened [i.e. in mid-summer]."

I sing of Artemis with shafts of gold, strong-voiced, the revered virgin, deer-shooting, delighter in arrows, own sister to Apollon of the golden sword. Over the shadowy hills and windy peaks she draws her golden bow, rejoicing in the chase, and sends out grievous shafts. The tops of the high mountains tremble and the tangled wood echoes awesomely with the outcry of beasts: earthquakes and the sea also where fishes shoal. But the goddess with a bold heart turns every way destroying the race

124

of wild beasts: and when she is satisfied and has cheered her heart, then the huntress who delights in arrows slackens her supple bow and goes to the great house of her dear brother Phoibos Apollon, to the rich land of Delphoi, there to order the lovely dance of the Mousai (Muses) and Kharites (Charites, Graces). There she hangs up her curved bow and her arrows, and heads and leads the dances, gracefully arrayed, while all they utter their heavenly voice, singing how neat-ankled Leto bare children supreme among the immortals both in thought and deed.
Hail to you, children of Zeus and rich-haired Leto! And now I will remember you and another song also.

—Homeric Hymn 27 to Artemis

There were sacrifices without blood, like perfumes, eating sweets, fruits, and breads. You can bring sacrifices, offerings, perfumes, sweets, breads, and sing and do ceremony. You can pray to HER here for your miracle.

Guided Imagery for the Temple of Artemis: Restructuring the Feminine Psyche with the Energy of the Moon

Imagine you are in the beautiful marble and stone temple of Artemis. You can see her statue and you can feel her energy. She speaks to you: Listen to what she says:

"You are you, and you are free, you are the instinctual woman. You are intuitive, and you still live in wildness.

You know all the animals of the forest and can speak to them.

You stand before the moon and see owls and the creatures of night. As you listen to the silence of the night, you listen to the silence of your own mind.

Remember... you lived like this for thousands of years... in past lives, you knew every tree...you understood the gift of each plant, you knew where the animals lived, raised their children, you knew the hunting ground of the owls, hawks, wild cats, and bears...

You are never lost in the wilderness... it was your home... a place of power and strength for you. Your legs are strong, your eyes keen.

Remember who you were when you were free and totally capable, strong, intelligent, highly motivated and full of joy in freedom and wildness. You were and you are now grace and power.

Now, take a deep breath, harness the energy of the moon and of nature." As you stand in front of the energy of Artemis, she points you to the moon, the moon sees you always, she is in the sky watching you, loving you, you will never be alone.

The Words for Power and Grace to be Repeated at Artemision

Piety and power - represents love of nature and worship of earth, moon, and animals

Passion - Feminine nature, the divine feminine is passionate about everything

Compassion - a basic feminine trait of caring and love, for self and other, and earth. It comes from motherhood

Devotion - to lovers, to deity, to beauty, to constancy

Attachment - to what she loves, duty, commitment

Tender Veneration - is a woman's characteristic

Benevolence - of a good woman, her endless gifts

Brilliant reminiscence - is her memory of the light of the moon, she carries this sacred memory with her always and derives her brilliance from it. Silver pertains to Artemis, shining

Graciousness - she is a noble lady, divine feminine

Regal Esteem - all the myths of the queen of the night

Flowing Balance -   She is always shown next to rivers with nymphs and wild animals near springs, bathing

Vigor - she is the huntress, always wild, jumping and running

Purity - her virginity, her unsullied commitment, and her independence

Chapter Twelve *Oracular Power*
The Monument of the Hexagons or the
Beehive House

Awareness: Oracular Power.

In Delos you become the oracle of your own life and acquire your own oracular power as you learn to listen to yourself. Oracular power is paired with the Monument of Hexagons because this very old building was probably the site of the most ancient oracle of Delos. There are references to the importance of the oracle in Delos. Considering the general scarcity of information either from the physical remnants or the written word, we would like to assume that for the ancient people, a stopover at the port of Delos for ceremony, recreation, trade, and consulting the oracle was a must.

The oracular power was an art taught by gods and required the knowledge of all the other arts. It is the king of the arts that uses all the others to formulate its answers. One needs to know discipline (that is mastering one's living time), one must be aware of his free imagination, know the crafts, and even music, dance, poetry, and all the rest. Your question could be on any subject and you need to apply the answer to your situation. You may like the result or you may not like it. Most people, when they don't like the result, dismiss the soothsaying as ludicrous. The oracle does not care, this is beyond the scope of its existence. This is the first obstacle to any oracle, and you must be aware of it. You dismiss what you are doing and you stop, or you continue. You need to use all that you know and feel to divine the future. The result should be something like jumping to the moon. The core of this book is to combine the disciplines you know and thus become excellent at your own personal science. At this stage, you can say you are an initiate miracle doer.

When you become the oracle of your own life, you can hear your own inner voices telling you what to do. You will not need to visit an oracle because you will be the oracle, and you will visit your inner worlds, your guides, gods, goddesses, and ask your own questions and get your own answers. Becoming the oracle of your own

128

life is perhaps the most important thing in this book. Delos speaks to you…you listen to your own inner voices being your oracle.

Positioning Yourself on the Monument: The House of Hexagons/ Beehive House

An artist's rendering of the impression of the beehive house as the sailors and visitors were coming to it from the port. This monument was built with white marble blocks and its outside walls were entirely covered with sculpted hexagons of a beehive.

The House of Hexagons, or the beehive house, is a very old, and beautiful monument. It is situated right at the old port where the ships were docking and right at the entrance to the sanctuary of Apollo on the side of the port. It was a very impressive symbolic and emblematic building. Each place on Delos has a mystery, each symbol is a mystery, and the house of hexagons is one of Delos's mysteries for now. In your imagination, look at this building. It was all marble, but all that remains are its blocks sculpted with beautiful beehive hexagons. Notice these blocks of marble with hexagons on them that remain on the ground, in front of the foundation of the building. What we understand is that the building itself was calling for the attention of the newly arrived, be it pilgrims, merchants, or seamen, because its construction and its beehive decoration suggested that a store of honey (or something of great value) was inside.

This mystery building has been an enigma, and despite many years of dedicated study, scholars have come to no conclusions because of the lack of definitive scientific evidence or writings. What is it? Archaeologists say they don't know how it was used, but recently there is a tendency to identify it with an early oracle. The building was a huge sculptured beehive, and it probably housed the information center or the oracle of ancient Delos.

The Myth Behind the Place: Bees and Oracles

ἀλλ' εἴ μοι τλαίης γε, θεά, μέγαν ὅρκον ὁμόσσαι
ἐνθάδε μιν πρῶτον τεύξειν περικαλλέα νηὸν
ἔμμεναι ἀνθρώπων χρηστήριον, αὐτὰρ ἔπειτα
πάντας ἐπ' ἀνθρώπους, ἐπειὴ πολυώνυμος ἔσται.

This ancient writing which is part of a beautiful hymn to god Apollo refers to the promise that Delos is asking from the mother of the god to stop her from being an insignificant rock floating about in the sea but instead have her become the place of a famous oracle and temple. Delos wanted to be stable, trustworthy, dependable, correct, rich, famous, and revered. (In exchange she would offer herself as a refuge to have the twin babies on her grounds....)

There are many references to an oracle in Delos since ancient authors always referred to Delphi, Didyma, Delos as the three most important Apollonian oracles.

The oracle in Delos has not yet been studied by the archaeological academy, but the evidence of its existence is ample since people believed in oracles at the time of Delos and Delos was the great sanctuary of the god of oracular power. Was it possible not to have an oracle there with all the stories of the three famous oracles, Delphi, Delos, and Didyma, and the significance of Delos? We don't think so.

The shape of the beehive and the hexagon pattern was the sign of Apollo's oracles in the ancient times. There are many myths about Apollo and the bees. The last part of the famous Homeric hymn to Hermes refers to the story of the brothers Apollo and Hermes exchanging gifts. Apollo got the lyre, and he gave Hermes in return a flock of three winged creatures who would fly and drink honey and make wax. He advises Hermes to respect them because they are teachers and have oracular power. Apollo said, when they get their bellies full of honey, the truth comes out, when they don't have honey, they tell lies. We identify these creatures as bees.

The Hymn also gives evidence for the presence of bees in Delphi, the place of the famous Apollo oracle on the mainland. Apollo advised Hermes to use bees as oracles because he trusted them. Apollo said that bees were the mediums of old, they had an oracular system that existed before even he, the god, was an oracle. God Apollo recognized bees as the first original teachers of oracular power.

Aelianus, an ancient Roman writer, said bees could foresee rain, cold, storm, and they were the oracle to notify farmers. In a time when the fertility of the earth was the most important thing in life, predicting of the weather was crucial, and bees were respected.

Apollo's son Iamus was taught to be an oracle by Apollo and became the head of the family of seers at Olympia. In the myth, he was nurtured and fed honey by two serpents when his mother abandoned him. Pindar said oracles were vaccinated with the qualities of bees, and honey was the food of oracles, the food for oracular power. Gods with greater oracular powers, Zeus and Apollo, were brought up with honey in their baby years.

The bees mentioned in the Hymns of Homer fall into ecstasy and prophesy after eating honey. This notion existed widely in lands of the eastern Mediterranean since prehistoric times. The name of the oracle, Deborah, means bee. Honey and barley flour were associated with the powers of oracles. The influence of bees in Delphi was seen and written about, but it may have been present at other oracles as well. The famous navel shapes remind us of beehives (these were sculptures called navels but in reality they were ancient styled beehives and were also used as the symbols of Apollo's oracular power) and existed in every ancient oracle. The temple of hexagons, or

Bee House was the original bee power place for the ancient melessa or bee priestess.

To the mind of the ancient people the Hexagon Monument was no doubt a direct reference to Apollo and divination.

The History of the Place

In Delos, the Hexagon House was a beehive that could be seen from the sea upon arrival. It was a visible beehive, a big sign that said, "Here is the oracle, a huge oracle, it's here, we are here if you want to receive." There was even a bench around the building for people waiting. Waiting was an important part of visiting the oracle. When people wait, they lose track of their body and time takes over. The people would watch the weather, look at the sun, the wind, the sea. As they lose themselves in the changing patterns, they become part of the weather. The process of waiting is watching the weather and allowing the questions for the oracle to come unbidden into your mind.

The existence of the oracle on Delos attracted many visitors and one of the benefits of this was the exchange of information. Information is power, and particularly in a time without the speed of communication as we know it today, any gathering of foreign information was treasured. Some of the Delos people became the oracular priests, protected and employed by the god. They would speak with the visitors, gather information, and file it away for future use. The information would cover a multitude of purposes, whatever would interest another visitor. Eventually the oracle business grew to great proportions thus influencing money, trading, and especially politics. States and empires were built on oracular power.

When this happened, the old beehive oracle building of Delos was changed into a larger, more impressive building within the sanctuary of the god. This change came about from the great power of the day which was Athens which, along with the profits of the oracle, would also reap political power from the trading of information. This new building was called Pythion, a word that would bring together the two famous oracles of Apollo (the Delphic and the Delian one) under the Athenian jurisdiction and their public-relations- minded political management.

There was always a question mark in the Delian excavations about a majestic big building built in haste during the classical period when Athens controlled Delos. This space in the sanctuary of Delos was only given a number in the research books. Its preservation state was more than sad and its beautiful white marbles were scattered all over the place; no one could say what it was used for. But recently, since everything else around it has been identified, we think it must correspond to a building mentioned in many inscriptions called "the Pythion." This word means the place of the oracle of Apollo, and it connects the building to the mainline of oracular activity in Delphi like a chain of oracular centers under Athenian management. The oracle business in Delos must have been very good to necessitate such fabulous oracular buildings. The old hexagons were no longer big enough for the new oracular activities, and the Pythion was the expansion of this business in the heart of the sanctuary.

What to Do Here: Ceremony

The beehive house or House of Hexagons was the house of the early great oracle of Delos, a bee oracle. You can consult the oracle there. This place is about Answers for people's lives.

You go to the beehive building, and you wait in line. The first lesson is for you to be conscious of your waiting, that's why there are benches; take your time, wait, and sit. Being conscious will come as you continue feeling yourself in the moment. If you need help, consult or be conscious of the words ending this chapter.

Guided Imagery for the
Beehive House of the Hexagons

In your mind's eye, imagine you are arriving on a boat in Delos. From your boat, you can see the island, you can see a house that looks like a bee hive near the shore. You recognize it by the hexagon patterns all over its walls. Because of the hexagon bee hive pattern, you know this is the place of the oracle of Delos, famous all over the world.

When you get off the boat, feel the ground and the warmth of the day. You walk towards the bee hive house, you want the oracle to answer an important question in your life. You see the house in front of you, its sides are covered with beautiful carvings of hexagons and it looks like a huge hive. Already you can hear buzzing from the energy of the oracle of the bees inside.

There are people sitting on the marble bench outside the building waiting. You sit down in the line, and speak gently to the people around you. The people move slowly around the building as one person at a time enters the oracle chamber.

You are excited and awake at once, you slowly drift into a dreamy state of not being ordinary, you tingle and hear buzzing and feel buzzing energy as you wait for your turn with the oracle.

Finally your turn has come and you enter the bee hive chamber. At this point, treat yourself to a honey bar. The humming energy is intense when you are in the hive. In the ancient times, the ritual was that.... Her attendants ask you to make a question in your mind. The oracle touches you and starts speaking.

You listen. It's the answer to your question—it may be a poem, it may not make clear sense, but you listen and remember.

The Words for Oracular Power

Superlative esteem - godly power of Apollo fusing body and soul, highest status

Delphic auspices - the acquired power from the sacrifice of the demanding pilgrimage to Apollo's oracle

Visionary mastery - far seeing mastery, gift of consciousness

Dazzling prediction - effervescent and alive. After predictions of the oracle, you are energized and full of life

Prescience - knowledge of the future, of what is forthcoming You can have the feeling that in your inner worlds, your DNA is rearranging itself, gearing itself for the future you already know.

Dazzling - electrifying brand new knowledge

Peerless revelation - unique, it's you. Your consciousness is giving you your uniqueness.

Inspiration - see your own spirit

Leadership - you are the first, you have to lead yourself, you are alone with your consciousness

Virtue - the right action with justice

Power seal - this is the moment of your decision. Seal it with your own power. It is a decision and a resolution at the same time.

Unique Disclosure - the reading pertains to you, it is personally done for your own unique life, enlightening

Elegant ascension - go back to the ship, don't drag yourself back, get up from that bench. Time is up, rightfully take what is yours. Be Conscious of your step back to the boat. Be content—contentment is the curtain of a well done finale of personal ceremony.

At this point of our sacred visits, you have seen the temples of Apollo and Artemis and the house of the oracle and now you can visit the rest of the sacred areas.

This is a map of the sacred sites in the periphery of the sanctuary of Apollo and Artemis.

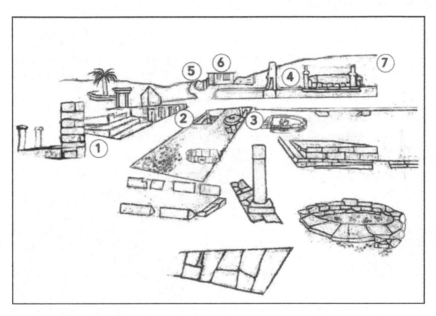

Map of the sacred sites

1. The way to the Sacred Lake and the lions - at the right hand corner of the path are the remnants of the temple to the great mother goddess Leto, mother of the sacred twins.
2. The Minoan spring or spring of rejuvenation
3. The tomb of the Hyperborean maidens 2
4. The shrine to Dionysus or phalluses
5. The path leading to the synagogue on the Eastern side of the island
6. The coffee house
7. The museum of Delos

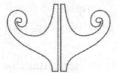

Chapter Thirteen *Creation*
The Sacred Lake, The Lions, and The Temple of the Great Mother Goddess

Awareness: Creation

Creation is the ability to reinvent oneself. Creation is the beginning, the light of the sky and the energy of the earth together creating life and change. The sacred lake is connected to creation because it is the place where the early community of Delos was first created and the place where the god of the sun, Apollo, and the goddess of the moon, Artemis, were born. The birthplace of these twins, God and Goddess, is the primal place of creation and for creation to happen. The god of the sun and the goddess of the moon made people conscious of day and night for the first time.

A Story, Coming Home

She walked very slowly towards the place she was told was the sacred lake. Now, she saw with her outer eyes it had become a place covered with a soft wonderful grass which made a pattern like her hair when she woke in the morning after making love. She followed ancient steps in her trance, she had fallen into her deep sacred space as she arrived near Delos and the island spoke to her. "Come home beautiful one, come to your mother, come back to the place where you were born and where SHE and HE were born." Her eyes rolled up and her feet followed the footsteps unknown and unseen to her logical woman. She felt and knew deeply that Her ceremonial goddess was emerging. Others around her could see the energy field around her flashing, its colors were like a light show. She remembered the simple instructions for ceremony in the sacred lake. She heard in her ancient memory, "Choose a spot near the palm tree where our ancestor magic spirit woman Leto birthed her beautiful twins, goddess of the moon Artemis and god of the sun Apollo. Lie on the warm earth, on my pubic hair and close your eyes. Let my healing energy come up and vibrate your whole being. Let the power of this sacred healing rebirth organ of the living earth, our mother, change you, reorder your spiritual DNA to make you again who you are, were, and will be to do it all and make miracles. When you get hot, it's time to rise and open your eyes." So, she lay on the earth like a newborn baby, like the one called by the most ancient mother. She let the earth cradle her, and come around her, and let Her spirit space cover her deeply. Suddenly, she opened her inner eye and saw her mother come to her and saw her babies come from her and it all swirled and she was home beyond any home she had ever known before. She heard, "Thank you my child, open your eyes and see the earth we have made, see it's sacredness, see you as mother, see your babies as joy and sacredness, see me as Her and see yourself as you are forever my sacred baby."

Artist's rendition of the avenue of the lions and the lakefront of the sacred lake. The lake was drained to prevent malaria a hundred years ago.

Positioning Yourself on the Monument: The Sacred Lake

When we talk about the sacred lake, we mean the green park you see with the palm tree in the center. It is round, so it is often referred to in ancient writings as the round sacred lake. It was a fresh water lake, but it was drained about 100 years ago to stop malaria that was making the workers in the excavations sick. When they drained it, it was filled with rubble from the excavation, and turned into the park you see now. The palm tree in the center of the lake is commemorative, it was put there 100 years ago to indicate the original palm tree, the sacred spot where the gods were born. You can walk into this park, there are benches and hopefully shade for you to rest. It's also protected from the wind. We urge you to go there, and when you do, imagine that this park is still the sacred lake.

The Myth Behind the Place

The sacred lake was the place where Apollo, the god of the sun, and Artemis, the goddess of the moon, were born. According to this myth, Zeus, the king of the Gods, had a love affair with a nymph called Leto, and got her pregnant. His wife Hera, Queen of the Gods, always jealous of his constant liaisons, was angry and menaced every place that would offer itself for the birth. The humblest of places, Delos, that was a freely floating island wandering in the middle of the sea till then, offered itself in exchange for its betterment. A deal was struck between Delos and Leto, so Leto boarded the island and gave birth to the twins in the round sacred lake under the palm tree. The gods were born and then the island was anchored to the bottom of the sea with chains of diamonds by Poseidon, god of the seas, under orders from Zeus. The place of birth is a place to consider any new beginnings, for the birth of a baby, for purification and for growth, for reinvention of yourself as a new person.

Here is the oath of Leto to Delos, from the Homeric Hymn to Apollo. Leto spoke winged words, asking her:

> *"Delos, if you are willing to be the home of my son,*
> *Phoebus Apollo, and to found a great temple,*
> *no other will ever touch you nor forget you.*
> *I do not think you will become rich in cattle and sheep,*
> *neither will you bear ripe fruits or produce abundant*
> *plants. But if you have the temple of Apollo Far Darter,*
> *all men will bring you hecatombs and gather here*
> *and the insatiable savor of fat will always rise upwards.*
> *You will feed from another's hand those*
> *who inhabit you, since your soil is rocky."*
> *Thus she spoke.*

And Delos rejoiced and spoke in reply.
> *"Most noble Leto, daughter of great Koios,*
> *gladly would I receive your child, the lord Far Archer,*

for truly I am terribly ill-spoken of
among men, and so I would be very honored.
But I tremble before this word, Leto, and I will not hide it.
`Too much,' they say, will the overbearing Apollo be,
and he will greatly hold sway over immortals
and mortal men upon the grain-giving fields.
Him I fear terribly in my mind and spirit,
that, when he first looks upon the light of the sun,
despising my island, since I am rugged ground,
he would capsize me and push me with his feet
on the sea's broad expanse. There a great wave will ever
wash over my head in abundance, and he will arrive at
another land which would please him to found a temple
  and wooded groves.
The polyps and black seals will man their
homes on me without cares in the absence of people.
Yet, if you would dare, goddess, to swear a great oath,
that he will build a very beautiful temple here,
first to be an oracle for men, then
among all men, since he will be many-named."

Thus she spoke,
  and Leto swore the great oath of the gods.
"Let the earth now know and wide heaven above and
Styx's flowing waters, which is the greatest
oath and most dreadful for blessed gods.
Truly, here will be always Phoebus' fragrant
altar and precinct, and he will honor you above all."

The History of the Place

There are two important lakes referred to in Greek mythology: one is the lake of the underworld, called Achcrusia (this was the lake crossed by the souls in the journey to the underworld). The other was the lake of birth, the circular sacred lake in Delos. Birth and death are related, both comings and goings. The first organized community in this ancient, tiny world grew on the banks of the sacred lake during the Bronze Age, about 4,000 years B.C. and possibly earlier.

This lake was and is an entry into rejuvenation, here you can be reborn. The sacred lake has special light and earth energy; it is a power place where your cells can grow active. Sun energy here is of excellent quality. It is the mother lake where the UV light and the heat of the sun are collected and concentrated in a natural concave bowl.

The sacred lake, other than being a stopover for the migratory birds flying from Northern Europe to Africa, provided for the community. It housed wild birds, reeds, fish, and wildlife. It was for the public. The lake was like a womb, it was the most protected place on the island. Sheltered from the north winds by the hills around it, it was warm, it had food, and it was a freshwater reservoir.[1] It was a protected place, not to be abused, dedicated to Leto, the mother of the gods. People went there to pray on the banks, perform ablutions, and make fresh starts. The lake became the site for life change, and rejuvenations. People would come here for rebirth, spend time on the banks, praying, dreaming, and basking in the warmth of the light.

You will feel the real heat if you stay a few minutes on a bench or under the palm tree, it's a healing center. Imagine you are at the center of a giant concave mirror. If you are conscious of the light qualities and your body, you can imagine you are there to reorganize your DNA, it's like reprogramming a computer. The sun's reflection on the sacred lake amplifies the brightest light on earth and aids the transformation. The intensity of this light, the poet says, was so bright it could be seen from the stars.

---

[1] Before the community by the lake of 4000 years ago, there was another earlier community that was lodging and protecting itself on top of the mountain. It seems it was safer up there since they could throw stones at any invader. Very old fortification walls have been discovered there, dating from Adraic times. We assume when they became a larger community they moved by the lake front. We could also suspect that by this time the new religious aspect of the island through the new god, Apollo, made the island safer. We estimate this was happening around 2,000 years B.C.

What to Do Here: Ceremony

It's that bright there....Go—sit on a bench—feel the dry heat (heat improves circulation and helps rid the body of toxins)—feel the warmth, it should be like being in your mother's womb. Expose yourself in the chamber that washes all the unpleasant sensations away.... And expect that you will have an easy rebirth...you will make it easy with all this energy. It's a place where rites of ablution and purification happen. Make yourself comfortable wherever you like.

The Sacred Lake is a giant mirror. The lions behind it face East, as if bringing in the energy of healing. In the sacred lake, the intensity of the mirror effect and the heat will help you restructure yourself, it cleans your slate and makes you alert. Consequently, here you will get rid of your body inflammations created by the diversity of acute feelings you have had. It gets rid of violent feelings, it purifies and polishes. You should feel like a clean pebble. You are cleaned up inside, cleaned up totally. When you are in the sacred lake, you don't feel like you want to get out of there, you feel like staying there forever.

When you are out, you see the difference. It's like a sauna with dry heat.

The best way to experience this is to lie on the clean grass, inside the park/lake or sit on the wooden benches. Appreciate your health. On the lake, you decide what you want to write on the clean slate.

Guided Imagery for the Sacred Lake

In your mind's eye, imagine you are in Delos. The light is bright-er than any light you have ever seen, the day is hot, and you are excited and happy to be there. See the island, see the white marble stones, see the clear blue sky, the emerald blue sea, the mountain, and the ruined buildings. Feel the ground under your feet, feel the small stones, marble paths, and soft sand.

Now enter the park/ lake, through one of the stone gates. Walk towards the center, the paths are there to guide you. The grass on the ground is very soft and is in beautiful patterns like the hair of a baby just born, it is springy like a mattress and feels wonderful. Pick a private spot where you won't be disturbed and lie down on this soft bed and feel the heat come over your body, it is hot and dry but you are not uncomfortable.

In your imagination feel the beautiful goddess Leto in labor. See her holding the palm tree in the middle of the lake as she labors and feel like Homer. Hear birth all around you, real and unreal at once.

Now, let birth turn into rebirth for you. Let your cells open to the healing energy of your own rejuvenation here. Let your cells restructure and become new and clean. Let it happen, the god-desses and gods will take care of you as you clean and open. You are totally protected and cared for like a baby being born.

When you are ready, it is time to stand up, stand up and walk to the palm tree in the center of the sacred lake. It is cool there by the palm tree. Feel the breeze cool your skin and put your head back and let the soft breeze blow through your hair. Your state of consciousness should be manifest and felt by you.

You are now cleaned out, purified, and open. You feel totally new.

All the worries, fears now leave you. You are empty clean and reborn. Open your eyes to the incredible brightness around you. You are like a fresh slate, ready to do ceremony in Delos....to fill yourself with the energy you need to make a miracle.

Go to the point of choice, go across, return back, and get a clean slate here. What you are learning is how you accommodate health with being. At the place where you feel the heat, you have to contemplate your consciousness is learning how to accommodate health with being.

Stay here as long as you need to, do not miss going to the palm in the center of the lake. Feel your rebirth in the cool air under the palm tree. When you leave, you are clean; then go to the right temple that suits your needs. This comes from inside to manifest outside. Stay as long as you feel you need to, it's the seventh heaven, the womb of Delos, you are reborn here. Rebirth is important.

The Lions

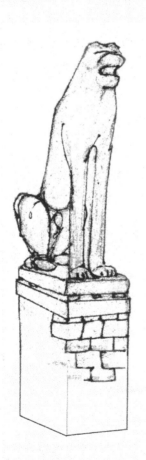

The lions are one of the great mysteries of Delos. They arrived between 700-600 B.C. and were a gift to Delos from the people of Naxos, a large neighboring island. There were between twelve and sixteen male lions originally, facing east and overlooking the sacred lake. The lions decorated the lake front which served as a promenade, where people walked, enjoyed the view, and celebrated the palm tree. In essence, they were doing what you are doing now--being rejuvenated and recreated.

The lions are symbolic of many things: they were protectors of the

Delos Lion - The ferociousness of the roaring lions still incites respect for the Sacred Lake where the gods were born

womb, the power animals of Delos and all creation. The lions face the rising sun, protecting the sacred lake, the new beginnings of creation, and were associated with the energy boost of new beginnings, sunrise, the east, and rebirth.

These lions belong to an extinct species called the Eurasian Lion, the common lion in Asia and Europe, which did not have impressive manes like the African lions. People in Europe and Greece, before the invention of iron weapons, were terrorized by these beasts. It was perilous to venture out of the walls of any community.

There is many a myth that tell us of heroes killing man-eating lions, thus liberating their city from the menace, such as Hercules. Herodotus wrote that lions were common in Greece around 480 BC, they attacked the baggage camels of the Persian king Xerxes on his march through the country. Aristotle wrote that lions were rare by 300 B.C. and by 100 A.D. they were extinct. However, ferocious lions were a significant part of ancient Greek lore, as their portrayal on sculpture and pottery shows.

Lions and Fragments of Others.

The lions you see today are replicas, the five remaining lions were moved to the Delos museum in 1999 to prevent further weathering. One of the original pieces was taken to Venice 500 years ago by Venetians who were passing by these waters, and it still now decorates the city of Venice.

The mystery is so strong that we don't even know how many lions there were. One story says there were twelve lions symbolizing the twelve constellations. Another story there were nine lions, one for each month of the twins' gestation. Whatever the truth is, they are mystical and beautiful, and when you stand in front of them, you feel power, elegance, and something more, as they invite you to participate in their vivacity.

Letoon: The Temple of the Great Mother Goddess

Positioning Yourself on the Monument: the Temple of Leto
Leto was the mother of the twin Delian gods. Her Temple is situated

right next to the sacred lake as we enter the Terrace of the Lions. This temple is one of the oldest marble temples in Delos. Marble shows the importance of the divinity in it. It dates from 550 B.C. and is called the Letoon. This temple was meticulously built. A marble bench was attached to the outside walls and since she was an oracle goddess we presume people were sitting on the bench biding their turn. You can sit on the marble bench and rest before going to the sacred lake and think about Leto, the mother, about to give birth at the palm tree in thc lake.

In her temple there was a wooden statue about 2.5 m high on a wooden base that was carved in a rough ancient style. Records show her cult image as sitting on a wooden throne, clothed in a linen dress and a linen drape. The story of Parmeniscus, the man who could not laugh, was about this statue.

The Myth Behind the Place

Leto was the goddess of motherhood and protectress of young children. She was a mystical goddess who became the mother of the twins, Apollo and Artemis by Zeus, the king of the gods. Leto was the daughter of two oracular Titans who were the children of the original figures who created the world, the Sky and the Earth. In that way, she came from very far back in Greek creation stories, even before many gods and goddesses. Her father Coeus, was the titan of the north star, intellect, and the thinking oracle and her mother Phoebe, the titan of the oracle on earth. Leto, as the, daughter of the parents of oracular power, male thinking and female feeling, was a powerful oracle and magical woman.

Myth says that Leto was born in Hyperborea in the land of magic visions, out of time, in pre-time. On Delos, one story told was how the pregnant goddess Leto travelled south to the island from Hyperborea, accompanied by wolves, where she gave birth with difficulty to the twins. The Roman historian Aelian, said, "Wolves are not easily delivered of their young, only after twelve days and twelve nights, for the people of Delos maintain that this was the length of time that it took Leto to travel from Hyperborea to Delos." The wolves were to insinuate the difficulty of the delivery.

Guided Imagery for the Temple of Leto

Imagine Leto , a goddess from the magic land of Hyperborea. She knows how to do many things. She is the wonderful mother of Apollo and Artemis the twins, god of the sun and goddess of the moon. Zeus fell in love with Her because she was so beautiful and she was a magic woman. Let her take you on a journey. She is a Hyperborean shamaness, a mystical lover who can help you leave your body and travel through space and time with no limitations. In your imagination, let yourself travel through space and time to anyplace you want to go… let yourself travel, she can show you how. Imagine she can show you how to be anywhere on Earth, to travel through time, and to communicate with the Higher Forces who created and maintain the Universe. Let yourself travel now, and go to any time you choose and find a magical figure who can teach you what you want to know, with her you can consult deceased spiritual masters and benefit from their teachings, find spirit guides and masters, and go back to where time was just beginning. Let yourself travel with her… now.

Come back to the temple of Leto, say thanks, and go on your way, a new person who can give birth to gods, too.

Hyperborea was a mystical land in the far north, possibly imaginary, possibly real where Apollo spent his winters. It was a land of Utopian happiness, no illness and eternal prosperity. (See chapter on Hyperborean maidens)

The fact that Leto was from Hyperborea made her supernatural and mystical, more than usually thought. Diodorus Siculus, a Greek historian from the 1st century, B.C., wrote, "The following legend is told concerning it: Leto was born on this island (Hyperborea), and for that reason Apollon is honored among Hyperboreans above all other gods; and the inhabitants are looked upon as priests of Apollon, after a manner, since daily they praise this god continuously in song and honor him exceedingly. And there is also on the Hyperborea both a magnificent sacred precinct of Apollon and a notable temple which is adorned with many votive offerings and is spherical in shape. Furthermore, a city is there which is sacred to this god, and the majority of its inhabitants are players on the cithara; and these continually play on this instrument in the temple and sing hymns of praise to the god, glorifying his deeds."

The land of Hyperborea is important. It is a connection to dreams, and the place of going deep inward in consciousness, like shamanic space. So if Leto came from there, it would be reason for her to birth these remarkable twins, not just a liaison, but a mission! She coupled with Zeus the sky god, an ocean nymph. Her mission was to make the twins. Apollo is an oracular god, he can see...Artemis is moon, it's all about light. Leto brought Hyperborea to Delos, to earth, to make miracles and birth goddesses and gods. At this point, we cannot overlook a reference to Stonehenge as a sun/moon temple far to the north.

Leto came from the mystical land of Hyperborea, almost a spirit priestess, and mated with the god of the sky, and only in that way could sacred twins be born. Leto was the bringer of miracles to earth.

Leto is in fact a mistress of Hyperborea and she controls the relationship of Hyperborea to Delos and earth. These myths are poetic and imagistic, the work of poets and playwrights. Throughout its history Delos was visited by innumerable poets and playwrights—one of them being Homer- who relayed their stories/performances and myths to the pilgrims and who in turn would transport those myths to their hometowns thus contributing to the fame of Delos. It was believed that poets and storytellers could communicate with the gods and were inspired by them. The myths came from the gods.

Guided Imagery for the Lions

Imagine you are standing in front of the row of lions in Delos. The sun is hot, the wind blowing.

The lions look east at the rising sun, over the sacred lake of creation. Now, identify yourself with the lions, feel their strength and power and courage in your muscles.

See out of the eyes of the lion. Feel the group of lions around you, feel their comradeship, their group energy, their beauty and power and move along with them.

Feel how lions protect their young, feel how they protect their territory. Now protect yours with your lion energy. Feel lion now.

Guided Imagery for the Sacred Lake

Go to the sacred lake, it's like a park. There are 2 benches and a tree. Do what you want to do... be you... feel the energy of the place and let it guide you. Sort it out, your thoughts, your energy, and take them and rearrange them into a new you. Take some deep breaths in and out slowly, be there.... that is emerging.

When you are emerging from the lake, be conscious of the wonderful experience you had. Be conscious of the new person you are and be conscious of the new resolved direction in life.

"It was a wonderful experience I had, I am a new person. I am a painter wanting to work."

The Words for the Sacred Lake and Creation: State of Consciousness is the Ability to Reinvent Oneself:

This list of words pertain to state of consciousness while you are in the lake, with the lions and the Letoon temple.

Manifestation - You are facing yourself.. all the thoughts are flying around. You are manifesting your real self, what is in your feelings and thoughts. You need to manifest your inner self with what you have now. Pick up these pieces, you can't ignore them anymore because the idea is your rejuvenation and reconstruction.

Epiphany - The moment you come out as new, the created, that is epiphany. You see and feel yourself as the new person now, you are out of the cocoon. The sacred lake is a cocoon, it infuses energy, it permeates all that is inside you.

Perfect accomplishment - Give yourself a kiss (on the shoulder or another place you can kiss on yourself).

Origin - It all starts under the palm tree. . Go there, take into consideration the myth of the two gods being born and apply it to yourself.

Archetype - You are brand new, you move on, relive your life with all the details. You know what you want, your DNA knows, you should know by now what you don't want.

Attraction - People go to the lake because they are attracted to it. In Delos some people end up sitting under the palm tree, that's all they do. And that's fine.

Revealing performance - That is what is happening to you, it is the performance of yourself, you never thought you would/could be able to do it, to come to Delos, to be here, to be reborn.

Initial consequence - is a performance recorded to be repeated. Remember the process… it is your initial beginning…what happened in that lake is the start. Go back to the start, see your steps, recount the experience of the lake.

Flowering - Enjoy the feeling of flowers blooming out, all around, like the lake.

Genesis - being born and being reborn.

Emergence - You are in the lake, you are emerging. In the lake you are restructured... and you emerge as a newly created person.

Chapter Fourteen *Fertility*
The Graves of the Hyperborean Maidens

State of Consciousness : Fertility

From the masculine sun and the feminine moon come the possibility of all life. Fertility is possibility. It is what is yet to come, the seed, the planting, and the energy of life. Ancient myths of Delos were about fertility, pregnancy and the birth of the godly twins. Delos was and is a place of birth. We pair fertility with the grave of the Hyperborean maidens because the four mystical maidens helped deliver Apollo and Artemis, they came while Leto was in labor. For thousands of years, the two graves of the Hyperborean maidens have been symbols of marriage, fertility, and sacredness. They are the only graves untouched by the purification of Delos when all the dead were removed to Rhenia, as they were still an active ceremonial site at the time.

The History of the Place

Herodotos the oldest historian about 500 B.C. (4.13, 32-36) wrote about Hyperborea, the maidens and Delos:

"Hesiod speaks of Hyperboreans, and Homer too in his poem The Heroes' Sons, if that is truly the work of Homer. The maidens are honored by the inhabitants of Delos. These same Delians relate that two virgins, Arge and Opis, came from the Hyperboreans by way of the aforesaid peoples to Delos earlier than Hyperoche and Laodice; [2] these latter came to bring to Eileithyia the tribute which they had agreed to pay for easing childbearing; but Arge and Opis, they say, came with the gods themselves, and received honors of their own from the Delians. For the women collected gifts for them, calling upon their names in the hymn made for them by Olen of Lycia; it was from Delos that the islanders and Ionians learned to sing hymns to Opis and Arge, calling upon their names and collecting gifts (this Olen, after coming from Lycia, also made the other and ancient hymns that are sung at Delos). Furthermore, they say that when the thighbones are burnt in sacrifice on the altar, the ashes are all cast on the burial-place of Opis and Arge, behind the temple of Artemis, looking east, nearest the refectory of the people of Keos."

Positioning Yourself on the Monument: The Graves of the Hyperborean Maidens

These are remnants of the tomb of the Hyperborean maidens #2, called Theke . On the left side a ramp will take you to the point of the nearest approach to the tomb of the maidens inside. Do your fertility awareness ceremony and invocation from this spot.

The two graves of the Hyperborean maidens were powerful ceremonial places in ancient Delos. They were Mycenaean (late bronze age, 1400 B.C.) tombs in the shape of a half circle and they were considered Abatons, i.e., stop, don't step in, no entry, they were sacred spots.

One grave, that of Opis (=wide eyed, perceptive) and of Arge (=hit a target swiftly), toward the port starting from the sacred Minoan Spring, This grave was an old Mycenaean tomb called Theke (hyperborean grave 2). Opis and Arge arrived first to help Leto with the delivery of Artemis.

The other grave, that of Laodike (public justice) and Hyperoche (excellence) was next to the temple of Artemis. It was called the Sema (in this book Hyperborean grave 1).

This pair of Hyperboreans arrived after the birth of the gods bringing gifts. No source tells us what these gifts were, but we know that they were wrapped in wheat straw bundles.

For the Delians the cult of these maidens was very important. Every young man or woman before marriage dedicated locks of their hair to them. The young men offered also their first beard wrapped in grass leaves. In later times, even today, couples come and cut a lock of their hair to have their marriage blessed.

Next to this grave (Sema) there was an olive tree. This tree was also part of a very important ritual. Every pilgrim arriving had to bite the olive tree for his protection and well being. Some male pilgrims would even go around the tree flagellating themselves. This flagellation was considered a great deed. There are two theories about flagellation in ancient Greece. The first is that it was a substitute for sacrifice and rebirth, the second is that it was to stimulate blood flow and health, like in a sauna. In legend, the original olive tree was brought from Hyperborea. The act of biting on the tree was a connection to Hyperborea, a mystical land in the north where Apollo spent his winters and the home of the four maidens bearing gifts.

About Hyperborea

"Never the Muse is absent from their ways: lyres clash and flutes cry and everywhere maiden choruses whirling. Neither disease nor bitter old age is mixed in their sacred blood; far from labor and battle they live." *Pindar, Tenth Pythian Ode; translated by Richmond Lattimore.*

Hyperborea was a mythical, mystical land in the far north. Boreas is the north wind, so Hyperborea was "the place beyond the north wind." It was a place where the sun shined all day and there was no disease, old age, death, or war. It was considered to be somewhere in the far north and scholars and poets have long debated its exact location. Perhaps it was England, the place of the Celts, maybe France, maybe far away shamanic Siberia, or possibly even the Arctic or Atlantis. It was a completely magical place of eternal spring, flowers, and visions. In the ancient myths, the Hyperboreans played a great role in Delian history. The Hyperborean maidens, the daughters of Boreas, the north wind, were believed to introduce the worship of Artemis and Apollo to Delos.   Delos was the physical place on earth where the heavenly energies from Hyperborean lands could exist, a special place between heaven and earth.

Eileithyia was the goddess of easy labor and childbirth.

She was also from Hyperborea and was summoned from the northern realm to assist with the labor of Leto the mother of the twin gods. The Hyperborean maidens came with her, passing from land to land and island to island. After the birth, the Hyperboreans sent two more maiden-priestesses, bringing gifts.

What is amazing is that these gifts kept coming to Delos from Hyperborea every year for centuries. We know about this from many

This is a graphic presentation from an ancient ceramic vase of the descent to Delos from Hyperborea of Apollo who holds his lyre and the Hyperborean maidens riding a chariot drawn by four winged horses. On the right side goddess Artemis holding a deer her sacred animal is receiving the newcomers. Note how the picture is full of the sacred symbols of the gods (sold as jewelry for you at our website). On the top is a line of quail, the sacred bird of Artemis, as if it were her guard of honor.

sources. These gifts came unaccompanied. They were forwarded from land to land and island to island as far as Delos. Perhaps they were following the old prehistoric road of amber from the North Sea down to the Aegean.

The Myth Behind the Place

The Hyperborean maidens came from the mystical north, from the magic land far away. There were two visits of the Hyperborean maidens to Delos. The first visit was at the time of the birth of Apollo and Artemis. Opis and Arge were said to come with Leto herself and helped deliver the twins. In some myths, they were said to deliver Artemis and then Apollo because the goddess of childbirth called Eilytheia was held hostage by Hera, the jealous wife; thus, they were like mystical midwives from the land of mystery. They were sent by the gods and were about ceremonies of childbirth, and sexuality.

This was a landmark transition—leaving youth to enter fecundity, entering reproduction, fertility, to have a baby.

Both grave areas were semicircular enclosures (abaton), and people would not walk into them, they would do ceremony from the outside. In early excavations, archaeologists found human bones there, something rare in Delos because all the ancient burials had been removed to Rhenia during the purification of the island. These graves of the Hyperborean maidens were too sacred even to purify hence sanctuaries. There were also found broken ceramic pieces, from Mycenaean times, ca. 1400-1300 B.C. These are indicators of the age of the cult.

What to Do Here: Ceremony

Since you know the myths and can see the maidens in your imagination, you can go to one of the graves of the Hyperborean maidens before getting married or being in a relationship, and the gods will bless you as a couple. Cut off a lock of your hair and your lover's beard or hair, before you get married. This was done in Delos for thousands of years. Be aware that this is the connection to deep sacredness in Delos, the visions, healing, midwifery, and spiritual gifts that are very ancient and beyond words and experience.

At the graves of the maidens, close your eyes and imagine your own connection to a beautiful, fruitful land far to the north, a land of gentle breezes and peaceful living. What do you visualize when you think of "the land beyond the north wind"? What gesture or movement do you make to honor that far away land and its maidens who generously attend childbirth and bring visionary qualities to our children?

Make that movement—gesture or dance, bowing or nodding, forming your hands together, whatever occurs to you—and welcome the energy of fruition and fertility that radiate here on Delos.

Make an invocation for fertility by the grave of the Hyperborean maidens. Then you cut a lock of hair. Ask for fertility to come into you life on every level, for children, creativity, and all you do.

The Words for Fertility at the Graves of the Hyperborean Maidens :

Fecundity - getting ready to have babies, state of consciousness to have baby.

Charm - is the first step (but it is only a step in a row of many).

Enchanting luxuriance - being overtaken by the beauty of the potential mother.

Fruition - overflowing with creation and new life.

Perfect profusion - that which multiplies as a gift from god and goddess.

Completeness - What is your path to fulfillment?

Progress and patience - virtues of midwifery and motherhood.

Miraculous abundance - (of babies and that which grows).

Benevolent endowment - the gift of being fertile and bringing new life into the world.

Lavishness - of nature's bounty.

Lavish flow - (of that which comes from above).

Increase - ...and multiply.

Ripeness in time - the answer to my death—a continuity to the future generations.

 Chapter Fifteen *The Source of Life*
The Minoan Fountain

Awareness : The Source of Life

The source of life is that from which all comes. Delos was the source of the god of the sun and goddess of the moon. Together they make light and darkness, sound and silence, and birth and death. All comes from this beginning. On Delos, the source of life is paired with the Minoan fountain because the spring water is the symbol of the source of life.

Positioning Yourself on the Monument: The Minoan Fountain

This very important water source for the community of Delos was protected to keep it clean within a building that is a ruin now. Everyone would come and get safe drinking water, the gift of life.

This visit was part of the general Delos life ceremony. It pertains to rejuvenation because the community of Delos was rejuvenating itself from that water spring. The Minoan Fountain was the first sacred spring in Delos. For the Greeks the gifts of nature like springs were sacred. They were inhabited by beautiful spirits, the nymphs, imagined as breathtaking young women. The Minoan spring was the central spring of the city of Delos and was the home of the Minoan nymphs who were the ladies of the retinue of Ariadne from Crete, thus connecting the spring to the Minoan culture. "Minoan" is a name older than Greece itself. It connects this spring with deep antiquity (3,000 B.C.E.). On Delos that was one of the oldest central places for people to go to and quenched the thirst of one, two, three historical millennia. The building of the fountain dates from the 6th century B.C., about the same time the oldest temple of Apollo was built. It is one of the oldest places on Delos as the community water supply was essential to Delos life. A flight of eleven steps on the south side leads down into the beautiful spring, so this allowed people to reach the water when the level was low. There was a simple granite-walled building there for a long time, and a column in the middle of the fountain that was supporting a slanted roof

The nymphs kept the spring alive, always rejuvenated and rejuvenating those who were drinking the water. They had their devotees who appreciated their beautiful presents of life and beauty.

The Myth Behind the Place

In ancient mythology, the nymphs of this spring were always beautiful and young ...and they got their youth and beauty from the waters of this sacred spring. In Delos tradition, the recipe for being young and beautiful was to go to this spring and visit its nymphs, but tradition also warned you, "never stay too long with these nymphs, they make you crazy." You could fall in love with them and lose your mind. Some people especially men could "see" them. Once they "saw" the nymphs they were seized by them and could think of nothing else. Nymph myths often had an erotic element combined with a genuine admiration for the earth of nature.

So, the Minoan fountain is about rejuvenation. People believed that the water from Delos and from this spring was active water. It was activated by the intense UV and by the power of the earth in Delos. And... by the person's beliefs, drinking it activated it too. It was a fountain of youth with rejuvenation and healing properties.

The History of the Place

All Delos took water from this spring. Once you were in town, you took water from this downtown spring. Its name connects it to the most ancient past, to the Minoan culture and Minoan nymphs, to whom the fountain is dedicated in an inscription. There were three nymphs giving water, and Minoan nymphs were ancient water goddesses. Archaeologically, its name, Minoan spring, gives us the date—Minoan times. It takes us to the palaces of Crete, 2,000 B.C., to the Bronze Age.

It gives us knowledge that there was a Cretan presence. Delos was an active trading outpost for Crete ("Delos was the seat of a Minoan trading colony."—archaeologist C.H.R. Long). We can imagine that at that time the first habitations, streets, and corners, were not scattered but were around and near this well/spring. The first settlement was at the banks of the sacred lake; this spring is very near the southern bank. This was the place to get drinking water since the well always had water and never went dry, which in the Cycladic islands was and is very important. It never went dry because it was next to the sacred lake. The lake was a natural bowl on the granite of the island which would retain the rainwater. It is now full of excavation debris, but the water is still in the shallow water table underneath, so it still feeds the Minoan fountain.

The spring was a great place to socialize, people would go there with containers and carry home the water. On top of it the sailors would get their water supplies for the voyage in goatskin containers. All the news of the town was exchanged there, it was the place where announcements were made, where people would come to meet lovers, to watch ladies, look at young girls, it was a place for looking at each other.

In all, this well has been the watering hole of the diverse island farers from time immemorial. It was the very sure place to get water, and the very place to exchange marine information, from rudimentary maps of the time to information given by the people who had the experience of any particular sailing and commercial situation. We could safely say that it was this well, this everlasting till today

This is an artist's rendering of the remnants of the Minoan spring with the statue of a rejuvenated water nymph rising from the sacred waters

spring, that played an important role in the development of Delos into what it got to be.

What to Do Here: Ceremony

The water here nowadays is not clean and you may not go down the steps to use it. You cannot use these waters for ceremony, and because the monument is very old you may not go down the steps, it's dangerous. Instead, for ceremony please use the bottled water you brought with you. Sit next to the top of the beautiful spring, have a sip of water, wash your hands and your face. When you bring the water in contact with your skin at this spring, you will get ionization of your body and you will feel refreshed and rejuvenated. It is the contact with the water that matters. That is what fountains are for. Each year Goddess Hera would go the fountain and return a virgin. This was celebrated in secret women's rites in fountains all over Greece.

The Words for Minoan Fountain

Rejuvenation - what springs and fountains do. You enter the
water, touch it, and you are purified and come out new.

The Fountain - the Minoan spring is a fountain, like the
fountain of youth.

The Source - springs are the source of life, symbolically and
physically.

Illumination - light comes from the center of springs,
it is pure white sacred light, it looks like it comes from
the bottom of the spring.

Fragrant Tide - what comes out of the spring.

Vigorous Invocation - the spring sings prayer, from the source.

Ascendancy - water springs out, ascends from the center of
the earth.

Inner Child - the ever living youth within you, your
inner child, who was abused and hurt by life, is
now washed and healed by this spring. You will feel young
even if you are 98 years old.

Blossom Again - being watered and blooming.

Sparkling Vigor - how you feel after your fountain visit.

Renaissance - being reborn.

Well Being - no matter who you are you need water and
purification.

Chapter Sixteen *Metamorphosis*
The Shrine of Dionysus

Awareness : Metamorphosis

Metamorphosis is learning or acquiring the ability to be another self (even learning to speak another language). Metamorphosis is change and transformation. Your life changes as it is born anew. You are like a butterfly coming out of the cocoon. Delos helps you become your authentic self through the resonance of art and healing. The Shrine of Dionysus is connected to metamorphosis because Dionysus helps you see and accept every part of yourself, your sexuality being an important included part.

For many people, dealing with sexuality or any difficult personal issues is like going into the darkness. This was *periagoge,* the long way of the soul through darkness into light, that Plato defined as the way to get to a superior awareness. Plato was a great philosopher who lived at the time when this monument was erected, and who most probably had visited this place.

This metamorphosis is a sudden transformation into another self. The new self emerges abruptly at the last moment in a process of recognition in which self-exertion is turned over into the other power. Till the last moment of the previous state, our thought is linear, stacking in line the rational thoughts. At the moment of change into a new consciousness, the rationality and linearity disappear and gaps emerge. At this moment everything is melting down and an entirely new self will be organized including the entire previous self in it.

Positioning Yourself on the Monument: The Shrine of Dionysus

The cult at the shrine of Dionysus was supported by groups and free associations of people. Participation was open to all just by joining. The theme was a social rite—a phallic procession around town. In the procession, there were leaders of groups, the leader sang a verse,

and the group followed. The songs were overtly sexual, with huge phalluses carried around, accompanied by teasing and dirty jokes. People around the procession would answer back with laughter and merriment. It was a form of teasing games, like theatre being played. The basic theme was, "I understand today is about your hidden other self, and I am also the other self, the sexual self that can come out now and be seen and see others." It was something like carnival where all would dance and sing together.

The parade and procession started from the altar and paraded through the city and ended in the theatre. They would put the big phallus in the center of the theatre and then the production of plays would start. It had a prescribed order, a rite, that would end up at thetheatre where contests of plays in drama and chorus were performed and would last for days. The participants were not only the inhabitants of Delos, but also the many visitors who came from other islands, the mainland of Greece, and Asia Minor. Wealthy people would sponsor the productions and invite famous international artists to come and play, singers, actors, dancers, poets, in contests between themselves. Then,

Remnant of the shrine of Dionysus which was decorated with sculptures of phalluses of all types and sizes and statues of god Dionysus and his followers. This is an artist's restoration completing a broken fragment of a phallic statue in honor of Dionysus.

they would honor the best ones with golden crowns and sometimes even statues erected to them. It was a great honor for a traveling international artist to play at the theatre of Delos.

The important part of the shrine of Dionysus is the phallus, and there were there the phalluses and their representation. These phallic sculptures excited everyone. Two large ones are in the Altar, and there is a collection of phalluses and phallic objects in the Delos museum. There are many phalluses crowned with flowers and decorated with garlands, wreaths, and crowns. The phallus here is the essence of metamorphosis because it is the other self. The phallus has two faces, two personalities, one up, one down, one transforming into another. The erect phallus is different from the flaccid phallus, as the flaccid phallus turns into the erect phallus when a man gets emotionally and sexually stimulated. It is transformation into the phallic self, in trance, that is the other self. People were and are still amazed at that inexplicable transformation that includes in it so much of the human personality.

The phallus as sculpture was a worldwide sacred tradition. The first sculptures in many cultures were overtly sexual. They portrayed women with big breasts and bellies and portrayed the vagina or the phallus. The vagina sculptures and the phallic sculptures had to do with sex and fertility, the great mystery. The menhirs, large upright standing stones, were being built all over Europe and the world. They were the ultimate expression of an erect phallus. The lingam in Hindu sculpture was an erect phallus. In India, Lingam were worshipped in ceremony with milk poured on them, and they were put next to a sculptured vagina, the Yoni.

The phalluses at the shrine of Dionysus were and are insinuating you to get excited (which brings us to modern day advertisements with sexual content and to modern day pornography). How else would you explain this, if you see huge beautiful sculptured penises all over, what else happens? In those days, life was short, life was harsh. It was cold, there was no central healing, it was wet in Greece in winter, there was little food, life's hardships were obvious every day. There was high infant mortality, more than half of the babies died before one year old. Families had many children to deal

with this, there was no birth control, society's urge was the opposite: propagate, propagate. The shrine of Dionysus was urging people to have sex so children would be born. Considering life at that time, Delos and its festivals helped propagation, encouraged people to meet and have a great time, forget hardships, and to do it in a sacred way: embracing metamorphosis.

Dionysus, the god of fertility, of plants, of nature's fertility, urged people to arrive at sexual consciousness. At the time of Delos, there was no differentiation, no rules, no prohibiting of sexual behaviors. Bisexuality in the pagan world was the norm, it was not looked down upon. There definitely were rules indicating and warning for excesses of the sexual practices. Many people were bisexual and therefore, we get Dionysian celebrations. In early days, the orgy was pure celebration; in later time with excesses it became different. There was no discrimination of what kind of sex you had, the availability was there, it was the metamorphosis, the other self emerged uncensored, and wild sex parties were sacred celebrations of life and the life force. When Dionysus was a mainstream god, there were no bans on sexual behavior; it was the opposite, sacred sex, trance, and ecstasy were the norm.

Women also were allowed to show their other self. The proof was in Euripides' play, *The Bacchae*, with women maenads and women ruling the show. Each person participated according to her own sexual desires. It was not all orgies, there was every kind of sex, private, intimate, orgiastic, all. Lesbians were not excluded, gays not excluded, bisexual not excluded. Delos did not exclude any sexual orientations. Every sexual expression was respected and accepted. There is even a statue of a flasher in the Museum of Delos next to the statue of Artemis and deer.

This chapter has to do with sex. If you are shown an erect phallus what were you supposed to think? Why else would they make a ten-foot tall erect phallus? Archaeologists say it was a symbol—but it was reality. It was the accompaniment to a sexual state of consciousness where you were encouraged to have sex for sacredly experiencing union.

This is a painting from an ancient vase of a satyr or a follower of god Dionysus. We see the extent of the metamorphosis of his personality.

The Impact of the Cult of Dionysus

Dionysus was a god as important as Apollo—but he was juicy, sexual, lusty, and in a trance, exactly the opposite of the sun god.

Like an actor in Greek drama Playing many roles by changing masks, Dionysus has more personality facets than any other Greek god. From an age old god of nature and fertility he became a god of ecstatic states of mind, and redeemer in after life. He was a god that signified change, metamorphosis.

Dionysus was the complex god of theater, wine, celebration, and trance. The animals of Dionysus, the tiger and the panther, are portrayed in beautiful mosaics in Delos. Riding panthers and tigers was the god of theatre and wine. Wine for Dionysus was about ecstasy. The Dionysian activities were the phallus, wine, the theater, singing, dancing, and ecstasy. Dionysus would help you get intoxicated and take the shortcuts to the stars....

There were the mysteries of ritual madness and festivals with dancing and celebrations leading to metamorphosis and epiphany. Frenzy led to trance and allowed communication between the living and the dead. Maenads and Satyrs followed him in ecstatic dancing. His mystery rites and cults seemed to come from afar. He was said to have traveled in India, the Middle East, away from Greece, before coming back. The shamanic nature of his rituals is clear: trance, drug states, music, drumming.

The cult of Dionysus, connected to fertility and wine, ecstasy and dance as a way to visions, was different from that of Apollo as oracle but had the same goal—visions and inner knowledge, investigating our human inner world.

The Dionysian symbols were the leopard, tiger, and panther, and the grapevine. He was connected with resurrection. His rites and mysteries were based on death, rebirth, and spirits. Dionysian rites were often involved with women freeing themselves from the constraints of everyday life. Trance also involved the bull roarer, drums, pipes, and were like modern rock and roll and raves.

When Apollo left Delos for Hyperborea in winter time, Dionysus would take over, it was the time of dreams, visions, and letting one core of the spiritual practices rest and be substituted with another. When one god was here, the other went on vacation and

This is a portrait of the god Dionysus as depicted on an ancient coin. He wears a crown of ivy leaves. His sacred plants were the ivy, the grapevine, and the pine.

the spirituality switched. As a general rule, in the oracle business of those days, Apollo's oracular pronouncements were given in the summer time. In winter time when he was in Hyperborea, his place was taken by Dionysus, and that was the time of visions and dreams.

Dionysus and the Theater

Theater to honor Dionysus, to honor metamorphosis, started as simple songs about the adventures of this god. Then characters were added, first dancing and singing stories of Dionysus, then his myths. Next, characters were added, actors were invented, more subjects were introduced, always dedicated to Dionysus and under the auspices of Dionysus. The goal of the theater was transformation, metamorphosis. Greek theater shows the tragic quality of life and its opposite, and it unites the community in a ceremony of emotional cleansing, edification regarding the will of the gods, and metamorphosis from an isolated state of life to an exalted community of initiates.

People started by drinking, they would join the procession of phallic floats, and it would all finish in the theatre where archetypal fantasies were shown on the stage. In the theatrical experience, people would see and imagine what would happen to their life had they carried out their worst fantasies. Queen Clytemnestra has a love affair and conspires to kill her returning husband, the king. A mother kills her own children to punish her husband's infidelity—these crimes were acted out for the audience to imagine, along with the punishments decided by the gods. Comedy and laughter had a place also, as an interlude or a relief from the gravity of the darker passions. And the laughter was always the criticism and satire of those who were handling public affairs.

Delos had one of the best theaters. The theater had seating for 6,000 spectators. This was an indicator of the number of theater-going people (everyone) and the number of visitors, which must have been considerable. This activity attuned to the Dionysus observances was an ongoing festival or theater contest, that would last at least three entire days, live with costumes, masks, poetry, dance, and song about the deepest issues of life, death, love, excess, and loss.

What Do We Do Here: Ceremony

The self that you are with your private sexual being, is the self you can find in the shrine of Dionysus. This is the self that other people may not see, your authentic self whom you find when you go inside in meditation, in ceremony, in sexual freedom. Metamorphosis brings out that self, makes you aware of that self ...pray for sexuality and give it time and patience.

> ### *Guided Imagery for the Followers of Dionysus and Ecstasy*
>
> *Imagine all this.... Close your eyes and feel all this....*
> *In your imagination, celebrate your body with the sensuality of delicious food, wine, strokes and caresses of most beautiful women or men.*
> *In your imagination, surround yourself with dancers, songs, intoxicants, passionate love, artistic dress, wild costumes, total creativity, and abandonment.*
> *Let your spirit fly in music, art, dance, celebrating your body in delight.*
> *Let Dionysus show you visions and sights, your boundaries transcended, total freedom of the possibilities for what life can bring you.*
> *See the women who lived in the temples, beautiful dancers, drummers, singers, delighted in sex skills, experts in seduction.*
> *Let them teach you the deepest secrets, take you to places where you lose control, are taken in ecstasy, go to places you did not know were even possible..*
> *All this is protected by Dionysus.*
> *It was drugs, sex, and rock and roll for spiritual metamorphosis...*

The Words for Dionysus and Metamorphosis:

Attraction - it's all about attraction, attraction to beautiful men, beautiful women, phalluses, bodies. We are born to be attracted.

Verve and Grace - are seductive.

Breakthrough - The emergence of the new other self is always a breakthrough, it comes from the censored obscurity out into the light of love, passion, and unity.

Movement - The other self comes out with movement, some thing within you moves. hormones, testosterone, oxytocin, estrogen.

Skillful distinction - Finding exactly who and what is right for you, only then could the authentic self emerge.

Sensuality - Sensuality, bodies, touch, the phallus gets erect when it feels like being in a new world that you knew was always there but you never visited.

Phoenix - The rebirth of the new metamorphosed self rising from passion fire.

Vital Flow - the exchange of energies

Equilibrium - Balanced outcome, satisfaction and calm.

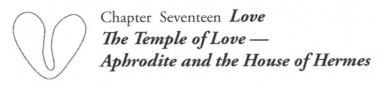

Chapter Seventeen *Love*
The Temple of Love —
Aphrodite and the House of Hermes

Awareness: Love

Love is the basis of all energy on earth. Love is the attraction of atoms, of the beginning of God and Goddess energy. Love is the first and the basic energy of Delos. Love made Apollo and Artemis, made the sun and the moon, made you…rediscover love in your life on Delos. Love is connected to the temple of Aphrodite because Aphrodite was the goddess of love, it was connected to the house of Hermes because people made love there. Both temples were places to make love and fall in love and by making love know love. Aphrodite is the awareness of the energy of bringing things together.

A Story: The Energy of the Sexual Serpent Arises

A woman tells her story of the Temple of Aphrodite.

"I felt Delos as the place of Great ancient Lovers. For me, Apollo-Artemis, were masculine-feminine twins merging into one. For me Delos was the perfection of the erotic male and female sexual energies.

I was aroused there, my body sexual and alive. I saw the penises, I imagined the ancient Dionysian rites, the erotic dancing, my body woke up and became sensual forever. I buzzed and vibrated on Delos, and I still do.

I saw the sexual sculptures in the museum, the lovers, the penises, the couples making love. I went to the temple of Aphrodite and sat on her altar and prayed for my lover to come to me and make love.

My ritual on Delos was to worship Aphrodite and raise the erotic male and female energies to lead me to my erotic divine feminine, to the unknown…."

Homer's Hymn to Aphrodite

I will sing of stately Aphrodite, gold-crowned and beautiful, whose dominion is the walled cities of all sea-set Cyprus. There the moist breath of the western wind wafted her over the waves of the loud-moaning sea in soft foam, and there the gold-filleted Hours welcomed her joyously. They clothed her with heavenly garments: on her head they put a fine, well-wrought crown of gold, and in her pierced ears they hung ornaments of archaeology and precious gold, and adorned her with golden necklaces over her soft neck and snow-white breasts, jewels which the gold-filleted Hours wear themselves whenever they go to their father's house to join the lovely dances of the gods. And when they had fully decked her, they brought her to the gods, who welcomed her when they saw her, giving her their hands. Each one of them prayed that he might lead her home to be his wedded wife, so greatly were they amazed at the beauty of violet-crowned Cytherea.

Translated by Evelyn-White

Lovers ceramic from Delos museum

'Shining-Minded Immortal Aphrodite'

Shining-Minded immortal Aphrodite,
I implore you, Zeus's daughter, crafter of snares,
Don't break my heart with burning
Pain, Goddess,

But come now, if ever before
You listened to me, from afar, and heard,
And left your father's golden house,
And descended,

Harnessing your chariot. Lovely the swift
Sparrows that carried you over dark earth
A whirring of wings through the clouds
Down the sky.

They came. And you, holy one,
Smiling with divine features, asking me
What is my suffering: why do I
Again cry out to you, now:

What it is I wish above all in my
Crazy heart. 'Whom now, shall I persuade
To take you into her love,
Sappho, who wrongs you now?
If she runs now later she'll follow,
If she refuses gifts she'll gift to you.
If she won't love, now, she'll soon
Love you in spite of herself.'

Come to me now, then, free me
From heartache, and win me
All my heart longs to win. You,
Goddess, be my salvation.
    Sappho, ca. 500 B.C.

Love

Alas! if I think of her, my throat becomes
dry, my hand falls back, my breasts harden and
hurt, and I shiver and cry as I walk. If I
see her, my heart stops and my hands tremble,
my feet freeze, a redness of flame rises to my
cheeks, my temples beat in agony. If I touch
her, I grow mad, my arms stiffen and my knees
give under me. I fall before her, and I go to
my bed like a woman who is going to die. I feel
I am wounded by every word she speaks. Her love
is a torture, and those who pass by hear my
lamentations . . . Alas! how can I call her
well-beloved?

    Pierre Louys (a French poet who wrote about Aphrodite in 1896)

Positioning Yourself on the Temple of Aphrodite

Delian Aphrodite, Goddess of the "erotic instinct," born out of the
foam of the sea, had a very old cult on this island. Theseus, the
legendary killer of the Minotaur in Crete, on his way back to his
native Athens took along with him the Cretan princess Ariadne who
out of her love for him helped to find his way out of her father's
labyrinth with a ball of twine and kill the Minotaur, a man eating
monster. When she left her country with Theseus, she carried with
her a venerable statue of the goddess of love said to have been given
to Ariadne by Daedalus. Daedalus was the architect of the labyrinth,
Greek culture's first great inventor, an architect, mechanic, sculptor,
metal founder, and a great jewelry maker. His fine works were called
Daedala, meaning impeccably crafted works of art. The statue was
kept in the official shrine to Aphrodite in the main sanctuary. Since
Ariadne was the lover and was the one who helped bring Theseus
out of the maze, she got to be Ariadne-Aphrodite in Delos. Aphrodite's deep connection with Delos was ancient and profound. This
deep religious connection should not make us forget the role of De-

los also as a port, a place where sailors and merchants mingled, a great place for love encounters.

The statue of Aphrodite must have been very old indeed and primitive looking. It was small, made out of wood, and it was finished at its base as a pillar. The statue was always at the center of a great deal of attention, it was overburdened with crowns and garlands. The feast of Aphrodisia was done every year (July, August) and we do not have extensive information about it. Judging from Aphrodite festivals in other sites off Delos, we can tell that it was a popular feast lasting well into the night with the priestesses, women followers, and courtesans leading the way in the celebration of their patron goddess. A new temple of Aphrodite was erected around 300 B.C. from pure white marble blocks.

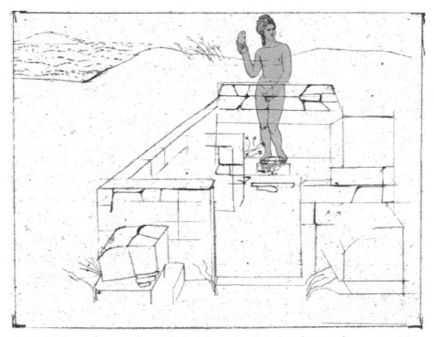

An artist's understanding of the Temple of Aphrodite and a statue like the one of the goddess that was within it.

In front of it, in the middle of a small square, there is the altar of the goddess also in pure white marble. If you imagine the temple of Aphrodite in its finished state with its roof and altar marble, it was stunning. Inside the temple was the marble statue of the goddess of love—portraying her dressed in a beautiful gown and wearing jewelry and large earrings, rings, bells, and so on. People would bring her ornaments and gold as presents, she loved jewelry and money.

Outside the statue room, at the entrance to the temple, there is a vestibule with two benches where people would sit and contemplate their state of consciousness pertaining to the goddess of love. Around the temple there is an array of different little rooms necessary to the cult of Aphrodite. The cult was an association of friends established by a famous family whose descendants kept it going for many generations, administering and doing the rituals, the liturgies, within the system of the official main sanctuary. At the entrance to the temple there are two marble bases for the statues dedicated to the members of the family that founded the new temple of Aphrodite.

Go to this exquisite ancient temple, which dates from 300 B.C. You can contemplate on the marble benches in the vestibule like people did in the ancient times and understand and experience the philosophy of the goddess of love. Go deeply and feel the state of consciousness that you will find here.

When people would come to the Temple of Aphrodite in ancient times, they would do sacrifices, place offerings of flowers, jewelry, and perfume, and they would sing hymns to Aphrodite. The singing and perfumes would put them in a state of mind of being lost in love. Swirling in passion and the energy of love. . . men and women would both be participating and this could eventually lead to lovemaking. This could be of two men or two women, any combination, all was possible here; this could happen when people were flying in the clouds of love. Definitely encounters could be made because the place was full of the energy of the Goddess, or you could fall deeply in love with someone you would meet in the spirit of this sanctuary. Also we have references of people asking and praying to the Goddess to have someone they like fall in love with them.

We suspect that if they wanted to express their love, the temple gave them the facilities to do this in exchange for favors to support the proceedings of the temple. Definitely encounters could be made because the place was full of the energy of love. People also went there to get back their lovers who were taken away by someone else. They made a ceremony and prayer for their lover to fall back in love with them, and have their love returned to them. This was the place where falling in love was sought and expected. Seekers were going to fall in love, find lovers, and thank the goddess of love for this.

Positioning Yourself at The House of Hermes

Advancing on the path towards the mountain, past the Temple of Aphrodite, there is a fabulous house built on the side of the hill.

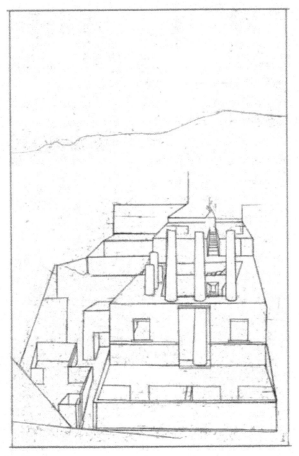

Visiting and walking about in the house of Hermes will give you an idea of the complexity and refinement of life in Delos.

It had four floors and shows clearly the way ancient houses are arranged in Delos, with the central area, the columns, rooms, water supply, etc., but this house does not look like the house of a private family. It looks like a house that can be used by many people because of its plethora of small private rooms.

It is a wonderful place to discover by itself. This is a house that has been partially restored, which is unusual in Delos. Here you can find shade, make a relaxing stop protected from the wind and sunlight. There are remnants of beautifully colored frescoes that indicate that the house was fabulously decorated. Excavation has exposed a spring on the rock where the house was built, and its water was filling a large cistern underneath the house.

This building has been called the House of Hermes because of an array of marble busts of the head of god Hermes found there. As a general rule these busts were signs that indicated very special places, in a way calling the attention of the viewer to the importance (social and definitely religious) of the place he had in front of him. Many say the House of Hermes was a house of love. This idea comes from its unusual layout and design. Possibly, if someone could afford better amenities than the rooms in the Aphrodite sanctuary next door, one could use this house for a hotel with more stars.

The Myth Behind the Place: Aphrodite

Aphrodite traditionally was the goddess of love, beauty, seduction and persuasion, sex, desire, erotic love, falling in love. She was born from the foam of the sea. She was also associated with swans, doves, sparrows, dolphins, seashells, and with apples and myrtles. The mosaic of the marble water basin with pigeons around it is the symbolic style of Aphrodite and is in the museum of Delos. She also was connected to Venus, the dawn star. Venus is the name of Aphrodite for the Romans.

Aphrodite was worshipped in cults in Cyprus, the place of her birth, and in Boeotia where for rejuvenation, she bathed in a spring accompanied by water nymphs. Temples with "sacred prostitution" and the term "sacred slave" characterized her centers, too, because many of her temples involved both falling in love and making love. She was married, one of the few married goddesses, but had constant love affairs and many children. She is the stuff of myth, legends, psychology, war, stories. She is about love, falling in love, beauty, temptation, whatever love and sexuality mean to you in your life.

The graces weave for her, wash her, oil her with perfumes, follow her with their dances. Contemplate various helpers around all preparing her to fall in love and seduce. Aphrodite had many children, both gods and human. Here are some of her divine children:

DEIMOS - The god of fear was a son of Ares god of war and Aphrodite. This is also the name of one of the moons of the planet Mars (=Ares).

EROS - The winged boy god of love was a son of Aphrodite and her constant companion. (Some say the father was Ares, others that she was born pregnant with this child.)

HARMONIA - The goddess of harmony (marital and civic) was a daughter of Ares and Aphrodite, born of their adulterous union.

HERMAPHRODITOS - This Hermaphroditic godling was a son of Hermes and Aphrodite. His form was merged with that of a nymph to form a creature that was half male and half female. People like this were considered sacred.

HIMEROS - The god of desire, twin brother of Eros, was a son of Aphrodite. The goddess may have been born pregnant with the pair, giving birth to them as she grew from the sea-foam.

IAKKHOS - A god of the Eleusinian Mysteries, often called the Eleusinian Dionysus or Hermes was, according to the Orphic Hymns, a son of Dionysus and Aphrodite.

PEITHO - The goddess of persuasion and seduction was some times said to be a daughter of Aphrodite.

PHOBOS - The god of panic was a son of Ares and Aphrodite. The other moon of the planet Mars.

POTHOS - The god of sexual longing was a son of Aphrodite. He was one of the Erotes.

PRIAPOS - The god of garden fertility was a son of Aphrodite by Dionysus, Zeus, or Adonis. Priapos was always portrayed with a permanent erection. The medical condition of Priapism where the erection does not disappear comes from Priapus. There are many priapic statues that were found in the temple of Dionysus which are now in the museum.

The History of the Place

Archaeologically, we should assume that those who wanted to participate would bring the goddess their offerings of flowers, perfumes, money, or jewelry to make her happy. In return, they would expect her graceful gifts—which would include the gifts of falling in love and being loved. The woman in Aphrodite was famous for loving money and jewelry. If you are invited to a party where you expect to fall in love and meet a lover, the consequences could be a love affair. Everyone came there to fall in love… they would fall in sacred beautiful love, find a lover, and then possibly make love in one of the array of little rooms around the temple. Some earthenware fragments with erotic decorations give us the sense archaeologically that participating in the goddess' rituals included making love under the auspices of the goddess in the rooms. This was not a bordello, it was a place where a man or woman would go and concentrate on the state of consciousness of falling in love, finding a lover, coupling, and generally not being alone.

What to Do Here: Ceremony

Go to this exquisite ancient temple, sit on the benches and contemplate the philosophy of the goddess of love. Go deeply into the state of consciousness that you will find here. Sitting on a bench outside the temple, find a place suggestive of the enhancement of love. Then meditate on the words at the end of this chapter to get yourself right to the point of seeing what it takes to be accompanied by this goddess.

A Story: The Journey as an Offering to Aphrodite

I walk up the path to the temple of Aphrodite after a long journey. For months, weeks, days, I have been contemplating on the mystery of this journey for me. I have touched my body, covered myself with perfumes, rubbed myself, dreaming of the goddess, every day.

I come to her, dressed in white robes, my ears wear gold. I am beautiful, on my forehead are golden jewels, I decorate my face with colors, my hair is gathered in wild shapes, covered in flowers.

I have come to become a maiden of Aphrodite. I bring flowers to her as sacred offerings. I am young, pure; I was sent to serve Her. I came to the sacred marble temple and now I sit on a bench and wait for the priestess to receive the offering of my love, of gold, of jewels, of myself.

She will come and teach me all the ways of the goddess. Before we go into the temple, beautiful priestesses wash my feet, take off my sandals, wash my body slowly in aromatic oils, touching every part of me softly.

After I am bathed, I am asked to sit on the bench and imagine what it is like to become the lover of a god. I am asked to imagine giving myself to Him, seeing him in His beauty and offering myself to him.

In my mind, as I put my head against the white marble wall, my body turns to crystal light, and stars appear, energy swirls, my body changes to light, all the colors of the rainbow flow through my body as he makes love to me, I let myself become pure light, I feel my body expanding, my consciousness balances and I am one with him..

The priestess approaches and invites me to come into the temple now. They can see what I have seen, what gifts I have been given by HER. One young priestess takes my hand, she is dressed in white linen as she takes me into the temple. For a moment I look out to the landscape and I realize that when I leave I am the lover, the priestess, the woman of wisdom.

Suddenly, I hear my voice in silence, I learn about my body by making it an offering to the Goddess. I am silence in this deep passion and sensual flow of energy. I came with the sacred intention to invite the goddess Aphrodite to come into me. When I embody her, I am touched, I am pure (I am conscious), my body is offered in reverence and every moment is beyond pure pleasure. Oh the Secrets I have learned.

Guided Imagery for the Temple of Aphrodite

In your imagination, walk into the Temple of Aphrodite on Delos. It is a beautiful marble temple, with an altar, a statue of Aphrodite, a waiting room and sacred bedrooms on either side.

You are greeted by beautiful women shrouded in white linen. A priestess comes and whispers into your ear. You go slowly into a trance and her face becomes the face of your beloved. You are so in love... your lover appears and hovers over your body. Your energy is pulled up into the energy body of your lover, translucent and shimmering. You embrace, you are the beloved and your lover, the loved. The goddess as your lover appears, your lover makes love to you. Ecstasy and bliss rise, move up out of your body and back. You feel pleasure, hidden delight, enhanced by your physical body. You realize that you have been in love from the beginning of time, to the end of time, and will always be in love.

When you see these mystical lovers above you, the Great ancient goddess and god as Lovers, you feel like they have come and are using your body to make love to each other again. You learn how deeply you can be in love. You can smell your lover's skin and feel her/his body with pleasure. You can feel your body rock, like it is in a hammock suspended from the sky. In the moment, your physical body celebrates from the toes to your sex to the top of your head. You rise and fall and hold each other, you become one and see the affinity of one soul. You feel the infinite delight of being in love and alive in a human body.

Afterwards, you fall deeper in sleep. Your Lover comes into your place in your heart for your beloved, you realize that you are never alone, you see the face of the goddess and god and become one, you give birth to the earth and to all creation. You are the source of everything.

Breathe more deeply, move, and feel your human body as a gift in this lifetime. Each day you will have your beloved in your heart.

The Words for Love:

Passion - the state of falling in love, this is the goddess Aphrodite.

Vital desire - you can't live without it

Heart's desire - this desire takes over your entity

Aspiring ardor - full, powerful, love energy

Fragrant potency - love, scent, and hormones

Radiant devotion - you become the transmitter of the goddess' love and it shows in your face

Radiant - filled with light from a divine realm

Joy - overflowing emotion

Rejoicing elation - elation from the beauty of love makes you so happy

Enthusiasm - breathless ardor

Heart's purity - the purpose of this visit (personal verification)

Twin flame - when you are one, a third personality emerges out of the combination of the two, that is the power of love.

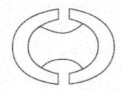

Chapter Eighteen *Protection*
The Temples of Hera and Isis

Awareness : Protection

Protection is daughter of consciousness. Protection is basic to health, transformation, and growth. In protection, we keep what needs to be in, in, and what needs to be out, out. We keep what is harmful to us, out of our body and our lives. Protection is a state of grace, a way of being in prayer. Delos gives protection by being so sacred a space.

Protection is connected to the temple of Hera and Isis because these important goddesses are big mother goddesses. Their temples give you the protection of the archetypal mother. These temples of Hera and Isis are the places of wife and mother, of children and family. Like a lion protects her cubs, Hera protects you and your family from harm.

Hera, Queen of the Heavens as painted by French artist Jacques Dubois 200 years ago

The path passing in front of the Temple of Isis (left) and Temple of Hera (right) continues to the top of Mount Cynthus. Notice the altar of the goddess Isis in front of the temple. Her headless statue is still inside (not shown).

Orphic Hymn 16 to Hera (Trans. Taylor) Greek Hymns ca. 3rd Century B.C. to 2nd Century A.D.:

O royal Hera, of majestic mien, aerial-formed, divine, Zeus' blessed queen, throned in the bosom of cerulean air, the race of mortals is thy constant care. The cooling gales thy power alone inspires, which nourish life, which every life desires. Mother of showers and winds, from thee alone, producing all things, mortal life is known : all natures share thy temperament divine, and universal sway alone is thine, with sounding blasts of wind, the swelling sea and rolling rivers roar when shook by thee. Come, blessed Goddess, famed almighty queen, with aspect kind, rejoicing and serene.

Isis and Hera

The temples of Isis and Hera are in a very beautiful place on the slope of Mount Cynthus in an area called "the quarter of the foreign gods." They overlook the whole island and the port, and from here you can see most of the ancient town, the main sanctuary of Apollo, and the sacred lake.

This place is about the energy of protection. It comes from the land. The Temple of Hera, the wife of Zeus is one of the oldest monuments on the island. The Temple of Isis was built right next

to it at a later time. Somehow one feels that the proximity of these temples has to do with the Great Mother energy possibly inherent to the location at the foot of the mountain steps.

The Myth Behind the Place - Hera

Hera was the great goddess of Matriarchy, goddess of the sky, the stars, the heavens. She was also goddess of Virginity. Every year she was a triple goddess—virgin, mother, and elder woman of wisdom, crone. Hera holds these aspects of the divine feminine for you to experience.

In pre-Hellenic times, she was the Great Mother goddess, she was synonymous with home, womb, temple, while she was the goddess of the sky, heavens. She was pre-Hellenic, far older than Zeus; she pre-dated him as a cult and her temples predated his. As the Great Mother, she ruled the stars, the winds, and the weather. Hera is the Great Mother and wife. Because of the special motherly feeling that we all know and have experienced, the awareness we work with here is the mother's security and protection. The atmosphere here is motherly love.

If Zeus was the king of the gods, Hera his sister-wife was the indisputable queen. The marriage of Zeus and Hera re-enacted as the primal couple of Sky and Earth.

In the patriarchal society and mythology of ancient Greece she represented the importance of the older matriarchal goddesses. Between Zeus and Hera there was a constant tension. This tension between the two strong powers was expressed with many charming myths about her jealousy over Zeus' love affairs, her schemes to achieve what she wanted to do, her abandoning Zeus for a while, and her conceiving God Hephaestus all on her own. At the end of these stories there was always a reconciliation.

Many myths show her as a nurturing goddess and a defender of justice. Other goddesses, like Aphrodite or Artemis, protected specific aspects of womanhood. Hera protected women in all stages of life: before marriage, during marriage, and after divorce or widowhood. She was the best friend of women protecting their rights, dignity, and well being.

The Temple of Hera

Each year Hera renewed her virginity by bathing in the spring of Canathus, on the Greek mainland. She was forced to be Zeus' wife and deal with his love affairs, yet through this, she was still a young girl every year and became a virgin anew. She was jealous and vengeful of her husband's constant affairs, but she remained the queen of the heavens, as was Isis. Legends said that the milk from Hera's breasts, while she nursed, created the milky way.

Positioning Yourself on the Monument: The Temple of Hera

The Temple of Hera (Heraion) is a special sanctuary that every city had dedicated to this important goddess. There were peacocks in her sanctuaries since they were sacred to Hera.

This temple was built about 500 B.C., all of white marble, and in it there were two statues of Hera. The foundations of a very small and very old temple of Hera (about 700 B.C.) were found under the pavement of its interior. In this very old temple, they had buried older votive offerings as well as a beautiful collection of early pottery in excellent condition, now in the Delos museum. This excavation proved that the cult of Hera was surprisingly one of the oldest in Delos.

The most striking thing here is the temple within the temple. A tiny old stone temple of Hera, which had a wooden colonnade around it and a canopy, was replaced by a new and bigger marble temple, as the prosperity of the island increased. (The sacred spot remained the same throughout the history of the cult.) Along with the old temple were buried its holy and by then old, outmoded, and space-taking votive objects. Such a discovery is, in fact, the dream of every archaeologist: to find remnants of the older building in understandable condition under the new one (thus learning the history of its cult) and to find also a great many of its objects from that distant past (thus acquiring art that belongs to distant periods in good condition).

The buried pottery of the Heraion was a collection of the very finest of painted perfume vases (and perfumed oils), statuettes of the goddess (it is from these statuettes that we can imagine the form and the looks of the two big statues of the goddess that were inside the temple), and beautifully decorated plates and trays on which they would make symbolic offerings of crops (wheat, fruits) to the goddess.

Every year at the end of August or the beginning of September, the special celebration in honor of Hera was held. The priestesses of

the goddess along with married women, her followers, would clean the temple and the sacred grounds, would dress the statues of the goddess and put jewels on them. The people would gather for the celebration, perform ceremony, sing songs, and as was always the case in ancient Greek religion, there would be a sacrifice of animals, offerings to the goddess, on the temple's altar. People did not usually celebrate inside the temples, those being the places where the gods lived. The rites were performed outside, which is why Greek temples are always more beautiful outside than inside.

The sacrifice was an offering of thanks to the deity, and brought the people together under her auspices and grace. This was also an opportunity for the poorer people to eat a bit more, since food was not abundant in those days, and meat especially was hard to come by.

The Temple of Isis

The Temple of Isis is a beautiful Doric columned building that can be seen from the ferry. It is one of the few restored temples so it has a different feeling to it than ruined temples with their marble stone parts lying on the ground.

In front of it there is an altar/incense burner. This temple still contains the statue (headless now) of the goddess. Around it there are the foundations of the temples of Serapis and Anubis, other gods of the Egyptian pantheon. A few steps to the left of the Isis Temple there is a small theater that held about 1,000 people, the religious center of the Syrians on the island. Both these sanctuaries began as religious centers of the Egyptian and Syrian communities (at the time of the "boom" of Delos, ca. 150 B.C.), but soon they attracted believers of different origins. In fact, they acquired such a following that the priests of Apollo declared them official parts of the main sanctuary of the island and gave them Greek priests. These foreign gods, with the passing of time, became more and more Greek. The cult of Isis was widespread in the ancient Mediterranean world. In Delos it was almost mainstream for about a hundred years before the island's destruction.

Here Is an Invocation to Isis:

Isis, please, only You can unravel the web of my Destiny, so twined and twisted together that no other hands than yours can know the secret of its disentanglement.

Please, tame the storms of my Fortune and check the harmful ways of my stars.

Sanctuary of the Egyptian Gods

Isis was an old Egyptian "mother goddess" and Sarapis was her husband. Sarapis was a new breed of god, combining Greek and Egyptian characteristics uniting Egypt with Greece. Sarapis and Isis were very popular at this time because of their benign nature. From the inscriptions found, we see that they are "listening to" the people's prayers; they help navigators, and mostly they heal the sick. Their specialty is eye and ear diseases, and Isis protects the pregnant women and children. The gods would appear in the dreams of the people and would tell them to make them offerings, and give therapeutic advice. In this sanctuary there was a special priest "explainer of dreams" who would interpret the dreams and the will of the gods. After therapy, the believers would offer to the gods "doctors' fees." In this sanctuary several votive reliefs with sculpted eyes or ears have been found which are dedications by the ailing wishing to be seen and heard by the Goddess.

Temple of Isis

The Egyptians residing in Delos placed the temples here because they are near running water. There is a stream called Inopos in front of the temple coming from the mountain area, and the ancients believed this torrent was a continuation of the Nile, and for that reason they made the sanctuary there. To the ancient Egyptians in Delos, the Delian little river called Inopos was just as good and sacred as the Nile. In ancient times, an Egyptian experienced a miracle there, he looked at the stream Inopos, and saw the Nile. Then,

the gods told him where to make the sanctuary. This sacred site of the Wife/Mother Goddess needed water for rituals of purification, and this place was about constant purifications.

Isis was goddess of the river Nile which flooded annually. Legends said that her tears for the death of her husband made the Nile flood, so as goddess of the Nile she needed water for the purifications and her temples were above the basins near the stream below. They also placed it high on the hill and alone.

Stand on this hill, overlooking all Delos, stand in front of the beautiful Temple of Isis and feel protection, purification, and beauty.

The position of the temple overlooking the harbors of Delos should make us think of another attribute of this goddess, that of "pelagia" or protectress of the seafarers.

Isis

Isis was the Egyptian mother goddess. She was goddess of marriage, nature, magic, and fertility. Isis in the very old days was wife to Osiris her brother, she was always shown with her child Horus breastfeeding as a mother. She was the daughter of the goddess of the sky and god of the earth, and she magically restored her husband Osiris after he was murdered by reassembling his body parts. She was protector of the dead and goddess of children. The name Isis means throne. In Greece, she was also worshipped as protector and mother and as the goddess of sailors. On Delos, she was worshipped with a triad: Sarapis, an evolved medicine god, and Harpocrates, a child god. She was connected to healers, dream interpreters, and she was controlling the weather. Plutarch wrote of Isis as goddess of wisdom. Many priests and priestesses of Isis were known for wisdom and healing.

Isis worship, in religions of the ancient world, became a huge phenomenon. Her cult was spread because there was a necessity for it at the time. People liked Isis rites and philosophy. It was a state of mind, and it was not only Egyptians who liked it. In the time when Alexander the Great of Greece conquered Egypt the Greeks appreciated Egyptian things.

These gods would also help granting favors. If you wanted a favor from Isis, you would buy an ear made of metal usually and make it an offering to Isis. That offering worked as megaphone multiplying the power of your request. This was called the well receiving ear of Isis.

On Delos, Isis became more powerful and was given a new importance when her husband, Osiris, was turned into the only completely man-made, invented god—Sarapis. He became the new and very popular Greek god of medicine.

The Latin writer, Apuleius, wrote in the second century this passage:

You see me here, Lucius, in answer to your prayer. I am nature, the universal Mother, mistress of all the elements, primordial child of time, sovereign of all things spiritual, queen of the dead, queen of the ocean, queen also of the immortals, the single manifestation of all gods and goddesses that are, my nod governs the shining heights of Heavens, the wholesome sea breezes. Though I am worshipped in many aspects, known by countless names ... some know me as Juno, some as Bellona ... the Egyptians who excel in ancient learning and worship call me by my true name...Queen Isis.

Sanctuary of the Syrian Gods

This place is immediately to the left as one faces the Temple of Isis, and used by the cult of two very popular Syrian gods: Hadad, god of rains, rivers, and thunder; and Atargatis, goddess of the earth, who was called "pure goddess." Their temples were shrine-like, and the rites were performed in the small (1000 seat) covered theater which contained the altar and the throne of the gods.

The followers of the Syrian gods were a tight community meeting often in their sanctuary for ceremony and for common meals. They followed a cult demanding purity. We know that those who visited the sanctuary had to be "pure" from fish (two days) and pork, from woman, from childbirth (six days), from abortion (thirty-nine days) and menstrual period (eight days). In return they had the protection of the gods.

These were gods who would help their followers avenge their enemies. A few prayers misspelled, scribbled on lead sheets (or leaves) have come down to us: a man's asking the gods to punish a woman who had stolen all his money, and a woman's against the thieves of her bracelet.

A sample:

....Syrian Lord, Syrian Lady, avenge, show your power... indict the man who took away, who stole my bracelet. I indict his accomplices, those who participated. I indict the very brain, the soul, the nerves of the thief and those who helped him. I indict his genitals, that which is useful to him, the hands of those who have taken away and stolen the bracelet from head to toes....the nails....of those who took away the bracelet of the accomplished....whether it be a woman or a man.

What to Do Here: Ceremony

The Temple of Hera and Temple of Isis are places to do mother, protection, wife ceremonies. In front of each temple there is an altar. That is the place to do ceremony. The Temple of Isis has the statue of Isis inside it. She wore a golden tiara with precious stones and in one hand had the good luck horn of plenty. You can imagine placing a gift or you can put a flower there. In front of the temple of Hera there is another altar, you can do the same thing there, place an offering, a flower.

You can also sing or recite a hymn here. Hymns were a way of doing ceremony and it's a way for you to feel the culture of that time. When the hymn is sung or read, the essence of awareness and the energy comes. You can get the feeling of the ancients by singing their feelings. You become godly in this way. It is an offering to the goddess for her favors.

The Words for Temples of Hera and Isis and Protection

Palladium - (definition: a measure taken to preclude loss or injury) The talisman of talismans, an object of sacred protection. This is a talisman to keep you safe. Hera protected marriage, she hated deviations. Also, a safeguard, especially one viewed as a guarantee of the integrity of social institutions. A sacred object that was believed to have the power to protect.

Shield - Shields protect you. The goddess Athena had a shield. This shield was a powerful protection.

Trust - social institution of marriage relationship.

Invincibility - you are protected against everything.

Immunity - your body's ability to protect you against disease.

Ampleness - Protection has to be big like the earth mother feeding her baby, the mother's breast.

Abundance - the mother's ability to feed the baby, the earth's ability to feed all creatures.

Blessing - the mother's love is blessing and protection.

Chapter Nineteen *Victory*
Mount Cynthus, The Cave of Hercules,
and the Temple of the Good Luck Goddess

Awareness : Victory = Achievement = Height = Whole Total
Point Of View

*Victory is change to balance through self knowledge, it is the biggest gift
of Zeus, the father of Apollo, the head god of the skies and mountain
tops. Victory in Delos was the opposite of victory in war, it was victory
in peace. Delos was a place of peace, art, miracles, and healing.*

We pair Victory with the mountain because the King of the gods,
Zeus, and Goddess Athena (goddess of wisdom and craftsmanship)
were worshipped at the top of the mountain. We pair victory with
the Cave of Hercules and the Temple of the Good Luck Goddess
because these sites are on the slopes of the mountain. The walk up
the path to the top of the mountain is the ceremonial way to victory.

A Story: The Woman Who Climbed Mount Cynthus on Crutches

*We (the writers) had climbed the ancient stairs that lead to the top of
the mountain. The stairs were difficult to climb, they were steep, ancient
stones. We were exploring the mountain top, looking at the temples of
Zeus and Athena. Now we were walking down, this was almost as difficult and challenging as climbing up. The stairs were so steep, the rocks
broken in places, it was like a staircase that had been twisted, broken,
and was almost an obstacle course.*

*Then we saw her, a small figure coming up. She looked strange,
like an insect, we could not make out details of her climbing in the
distance. As she approached, we could see that she was on crutches. We
had difficulty climbing, and we could walk well, and here was a woman
climbing with two crutches. We were amazed and stood there, to the side
of the stone steps watching her climb up.*

*When she was next to us, we said hello and talked. We told her that
it was very brave of her to attempt this mountain staircase on crutches.
She was in fact, almost at the top now. She had achieved victory.*

She told us, "I was in a horrible accident several years ago. Many bones in my body were broken, and I could not walk for years. I had to learn to walk and from this I learned many things in life. I had been to Delos before and had been changed by my visit. I knew once I learned to walk again, I would return to Delos, and I would climb the mountain for my victory over this accident and event in my life. All through my rehabilitation, I held Delos in my mind as my teacher and my goal for healing. Delos helped me heal, helped my spirit rise in times of tragedy, and made me smile in times of tears. And now I am almost at the top, I am so proud, happy, and full of achievement. Thank you Delos for this." We continued our walk, really amazed and healed ourselves by this experience. It was indeed fantastic that this amazing woman could have done this, could do this, and we applauded her.

Ancient stone stairs to the top of Mount Cynthus

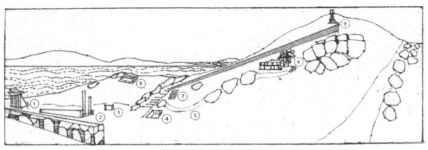

Path ascending to the sacred mountain

Positioning Yourself on the Monument: The Mountain Area

1. Temple of Isis
2. Temple of Hera
3. Altar to the temple of Hera
4. Fountain of purification preparing for the ascent
5. Path to the Cave of Hercules
6. Cave of Mt. Cynthus and Temple of Hercules
7. Temple of Good Luck Goddess
8. Temple of Artemis protectress of pregnancy and childbirth
9. Mountaintop temples to Zeus god of the skies and Athena
    goddess of wisdom

The top of Mount Cynthus is the first place inhabited by the earliest settlers on Delos. There were three stone staircase paths that led to the top of the mountain. The main one that can be seen is in very good condition, the other two on either side of it can be seen but are not in condition for climbing. (Please do not use them, use the main one that you can see.) On the very first step of the path you can see a water reservoir for ablutions when one would start climbing. This is the first step to victory: purify yourself. Opposite this ablution cistern, there are two words carved on the rock: they indicate that the rock is a shrine to goddess Athena instigator of craftsmanship. The second step to victory is that you will need her qualities, which are wisdom and craftsmanship. The ancient holy way steps continue towards the top. Ten steps further up there is a path that goes to the right up to the cave of Cynthus, shrine to Hercules. Hikers love the mountain because it's a climb. Each day you see young and old walking up.

After the path to the cave of Cynthus, continue up the staircase until it angles to the right. This angle has two sides, an inside angle and outside angle. If you look into the inside angle, you will see the remnants of the Temple of the Good Luck Goddess. On the outside of the angle, if you look to the top of the nearest visible hill, you can see the remnants of the Temple of Goddess Artemis, as giver of easy childbirth. This little temple called the Artemis Lochia Temple was famous in antiquity and referenced by many ancient writers as the favorite pilgrimage spot of pregnant women.

Continuing up the steps to the top, you get to go to the temples of Zeus Cynthius (called like this because of the name of the mountain, Mt. Cynthus. "Cynthus" is a word that belongs to a group of words that originate from the "pre-Hellenic" times, that is the times before what we call a Greek identity was culturally established. It is an old word, its meaning lost in the depths of time) and Athena Cynthia (called like this for the same reason). The modern name Cynthia, given to many girls, means "the girl dedicated to Mt. Cynthus," and many women named Cynthia visit this mountain today.

The Cynthion, or the sanctuary sacred to Athena Cynthia and Zeus Cynthius, was located at the highest point of the island, on a platform. It was always a sacred spot. The Sanctuary of Athena Cynthia and Zeus Cynthius had majestic staircases for entry into the sacred precinct. The Cynthion was on a square, raised site supported by huge granite retaining walls. Two rectangular buildings were the Temples of the Gods surrounded by walls enclosing the sacred area. From this spectacular place, you can see practically all of the Cycladic islands and further from its 360-degree view.

The top of Mount Cynthus is the place that brings in the light, that brings the victorious consciousness of achievement into you. Open your arms up and you will see it. You can see all of Delos, and the surrounding islands. From this victorious point, you can now choose the correct direction you have been wanting—literally and symbolically.

Positioning Yourself on the Mountain Area: The Cave of Cynthus, or the Shrine to Hercules, or Possibly the Site of the Early Oracle

The Cave of Cynthus is one of the most beautiful places in Delos. It is a primitive-looking cave of balanced rocks halfway up mount Cynthus. It was theorized that that the cave on Cynthus was a primitive temple. An early French School researcher M. Lebegue wrote this:

"An altar in the open air; then a roof to shelter the altar, next, a door to keep out the profane; lastly, a precinct added to the house of the god. This temple was the seat of an oracle. The presence of the cleft for water in such a cavern would of itself make this almost certain. The grotto on Cynthus is analogous in this respect to the adyton at Delphi, the cave of the Clarian Apollo, the cave of Trophonius, the shrines of the Sibyl at Cumae and Lilybaeum, the oracle of the earth in Elis, with many more that could be named. We need not lay stress on the probable presence of tripod and cortina.

"The whole character of the grotto proves, however, that it must have been used as a temple long before such Greek art existed. We have mentioned the enormous block of granite in which the pedestal of the statue was set. This block was probably one of those stones which were worshipped as having fallen from heaven, or as emblems of gods. It may have symbolized the god originally worshipped in the grotto, before the days of even archaic sculpture. The baetyl and the later statue probably represented different gods. But they may have represented the same god, just as stones (ireTpat), said to have fallen from heaven, were worshipped in the ancient temple of the Ochomenian Charites (= graces) conjointly."

There are other theories about the cave, some thought the god Apollo and goddess Artemis were born in the cave, some thought it was a temple of Apollo or Hercules. Some thought it was the most ancient place on Delos, others, it was more recent. Whatever the theory, it is sacred, beautiful, and special. For that very reason it is up to you to enjoy yourself and identify this temple with your inner understanding of yourself, thus give sacred realization to your innermost existence.

The cave is a place to do ceremony, make offerings, rest in the cool shade (rare on Delos) without people. Almost no one comes to the cave. It is an ancient and sacred place. This ancient place has definitely been used as such from time immemorial. During its historical life, it went through many construction alterations, and we can see its last phase as a temple to Hercules when the Herculean roof rocks were placed (style of the construction coincides with the qualities of this god) along with a large statue of Hercules that could be seen from afar. It had a round marble base that is still there.

This is a mosaic floor inscription at the entrance of the Sanctuaries at the top of Mount Cynthus identifying securely the places of cult.

Understanding the Topography of Mt. Cynthus

The sacred mountain, Kynthos in Greek, is 112 meters high (424 feet). It was dedicated to Zeus, head of the Greek gods and his daughter Goddess Athena goddess of Wisdom.

Mountaintops were dedicated to Zeus, god of the skies, clouds, rain, and thunderbolts. A special cult was celebrated at the sanctuary on the top of this mountain which was called the "Cynthion." In its temples (architectural remnants of which can be seen scattered on the flanks) there were the statues of Zeus and his daughter Athena, goddess of wisdom, as well as sacred paintings hung on the walls, which were votive offerings. In the yearly celebrations, adolescents (ephebes) would participate in torch-bearing courses and race to the top in the night, finishing at the altar of the temple. In ancient times, these torch bearing contests at night should have been quite impressive in the darkness. There would be offerings, and the cult's followers (initiates) would participate in special ritual banquets.

Orientals from among Delos' international residents were attracted to the mountaintop because their gods were "gods of the high mountains." Some of these Orientals were initiated into the Zeus Kynthios cult. Some of them built, farther along the mountain top, a small temple to Zeus Hypsistos ("Zeus, the Highest One") which was a Greek name for their oriental god, Baal.

An image of Zeus god of the skies with his favorite bird, the eagle.

Athena, goddess of wisdom and craftmanship had her temple on top of the mountain.

It is on this mountain top that the first inhabitants of the island had lived. Remnants of the foundations of the twelve stone huts were found, from the first organized community of the island, about 3,000 B.C. The mountain made a good observation post: it gave them protection, and they could always defend themselves by hurling rocks at looting attackers.

Map of the Cyclades and the Islands of the Aegean

Standing at the top of the sacred mountain, Kynthos you can see all the islands which constitute the central Aegean group called the Cyclades, because they form a circle around Delos. On a clear day many of the Cyclades can be seen; pick them out, one by one, at the other end of island channels, behind other islands, one fading behind another melting into the horizon. Delos stands in the middle of this lovely group. This central position of Delos surely had something to do with turning the island into a religious and commercial hub. Inevitably the "heart" of the Cyclades was seen as something special, sacred.

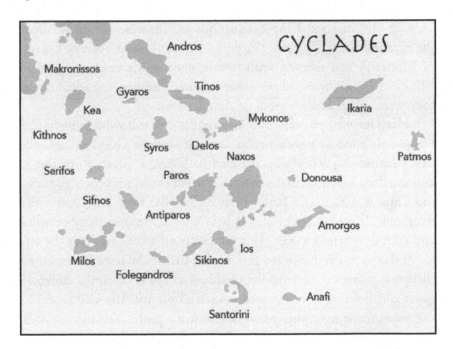

The Temple of the Good Luck Goddess

Arsinoe, the Good Luck Goddess, was Queen of Thrace, Egypt, and more. She was daughter of Ptolemy First, the king of Egypt when it was a Greek state (after Egypt was conquered by Alexander the Great of Greece) and she got married to three kings. When she was

This is the coin minted by queen Arsenoe (275 B.C.) who was the personification of Good Luck Goddess since she became a queen three times in her lifetime. On one side we see her portrait and on the other side the horns of plenty.

only 15 she married King Lysimachus of Thrace. When he died, she married her half-brother Ptolemy Keraunos and become Queen of Macedon and Thrace, with power over south Greece and Asia Minor. She next married her other brother Ptolemy the Second and they were called Philadelphoi (sibling lovers).

Her face was put on coins and had a cult following and finally was worshipped as a goddess. So Arsinoe was the Good Luck Goddess because she was always married to kings, a queen three times, and she demonstrated that a mortal woman could become a goddess, too! She was rich and famous, an early superstar. She was luck's daughter all over Greece, and that is why there are many temples and shrines devoted to her. Her temple is off to the right, at the angle of the steps up the sacred mountain. Inside the temple, we know there was a marble statue of the Goddess of Luck wearing a crown of gems and holding a scepter and a horn of plenty. The visit is seeing the monument from the corner of the stone path. You cannot walk into this temple since it is full of thorn bushes. Throw a coin for ceremony from the path.

What to Do Here: The Ceremony Is Going up the Path

A fragmented inscription was found telling us about the ancient ceremony of climbing Mount Cynthus. "...to go to the sanctuary of

Zeus Kynthios and Athena Kynthia having the hands and the soul pure, being dressed in white, without shoes, having abstained from sex and meat; to be carrying nothing, neither a key nor an iron ring, nor a belt, nor a purse, nor arms of war; to do none of the prohibited things; to do the sacrifices according to the ancestral customs…" You can take this ancient Greek text to heart as much as you wish.

For you, the ceremony of climbing the Mount Cynthus includes:

1. Going up. (Maybe you don't even go there on your first visit to Delos, you go on your second visit. The hike is long and steep and it takes 20 -30 minutes to go up or down. The visit to Delos is long, it takes much longer than a couple of hours. This book pertains to more than one visit, and you have your own choice of what to visit after you read it.

You can't really see the mountain and cave and the rest of Delos in one visit, so it's a choice. Several visits to Delos are important, you can't do ceremony and feel all twelve places in one visit. You should choose one or two, or even just walk and feel it the first time, follow your feet and your heart.)

2. Having water ablutions at the beginning at the sacred cistern of the goddess of craftsmanship Athena (her name is scribbled on the granite rock opposite to the ablutions cistern from the time the Greek alphabet was invented).

3. Visiting the cave of Cynthus, the Temple of Hercules, the hero of strength and perseverance, always helping mankind from dangers.

4. Making a right turn upwards with the consciousness of the Good Luck Goddess whose temple is exactly there…,

5. Making a left turn upwards with the consciousness of Artemis the goddess of childbirth for a good pregnancy and labor.

6. And finally arriving at the top, at Zeus' temple and his daughter Athena's wisdom temple.

The ceremony is a sacred pilgrimage to a temple of Zeus and Athena, for victory, achievement, and wisdom. It is done to change your life. You make your own ceremony in the cave and at the top of the mountain. Let your heart speak to you…

Going up the mountain is a hike in the sun and wind, you are climbing ancient steps with a stop at the temple of the Good Luck Goddess and at the cave. You will do something different in each place since each one is a pilgrimage in itself.

The cave is an altar, it is the place for gifts, for you to give an offering and rest in the shade. The altar is a wonderful place to talk, chant, give offerings to gods and goddesses, offer yourself and others, a place to eat and drink.

When you climb the mountain and go to the cave, there is a feeling that there is nothing like it, you can't explain it.

Starting to climb and having begun with a rite of purification with some water (from your bottle), you then think about wisdom. Approach the mountain step by step, breathing with mindfulness, as a way to consciousness. Breathing underlies all control—breathe on the top in all directions for wisdom. It is the throne of your having been there and conquered the greatest beast—yourself. It is your victory to understand yourself and to know all the directions of wisdom.

Victory is a new start. In every healing, there is a new start. You cannot begin a healing without a brand new start. At the top, you begin healing in all directions, in all 360 degrees. That is how problems are solved, you choose one direction, that is victory and you are the victor—"I am the one who knows where to go next." For some people, it is a personal sacrifice, an effort to climb. Your sacrifice is not killing an animal, it's doing a walk that takes stamina in the wind and heat. It is about not being belligerent but being totally pure. That is why you carry no metal, and you wear white. You need to give up to be the victor since victory is letting go of ego.

A Story: My Ceremony in the Cave

A woman tells her story of going to the cave and doing ceremony:

I bought flowers in Mykonos and food. I went to Delos for a sacred pilgrimage, I said I am going to have a transformative experience, where I would bring my darkness and my burdens, where I could think about them.

I came to make an offering in a temple, I wanted to leave a gift. I wanted to make an offering of myself. I knew that in Delos, you try to find your place, you are lost, there are many paths.

I found this old temple, in a cave. It was like a threshold for me, I called names and did a ceremony about what I wanted to let go of.

I made an altar with water, flowers, to put something to let go of, I said Delos will take it, let go of fear, give myself as offering, feel the energy come up from the earth, feel the connection of earth and sky, feel my heart opening and being full of the light of Delos—feel the light of Delos and feel my body transformed. I let go of something I needed to lose.

Then I left…I went to the top of the mountain and realized with each step who I was, then I brought in the light. I felt like I could see the whole Mediterranean, I felt this energy bring in light and peace. I said, Allow the light to enter the top of my head, that is all I had to do there.

The cave on Mount Cynthus

The Words for the Mountain and Victory:

Luck - is unpredictable.

Sacrifice - what you leave behind …so you win what there is ahead.

Perseverance - you need it to do your climb

Satisfaction - victory, achievement you are there.

Noblesse - comes from cleansing: no metals, no weapons, being cultured refined, being in control of one's functions—body, mind, and spirit. Here it is an aesthetic concept whereupon you feel squeaky clean— spotless and pure. That is why you wear white, no rough stuff, metals, or weapons. That is the feeling when you enter the temples at the top.

Advance - you move in your life from one place to a higher place

Success - you have achieved your consciousness and rebirth and your miracle.

Applause - people are conscious of what you did, they feel it and their applause does not interest you any more.

Throne - of Zeus on mountain top

Goddess Victory crowning a winner

Chapter Twenty *Health*
The Temple of Asclepius

Awareness: Health

Health in Delos is a total sense of balance and wellbeing. Health is connected to the temple of Asclepius because Asclepius, son of Apollo, was the healing God of Greece. His father Apollo taught him medicine so the medicine of Asclepius was the medicine of the gods and came from Delos.

Seeing the healing god Asclepius in his hospital was healing. The miracles in Delos were profound and involved more than physical healing. It was about healing your whole life and participating in the life of your culture. In Delos, this meant doing ceremony, visiting the monuments, going to the theater, all. Delos was the major art healing site in the western world for many centuries.

Positioning Yourself on the Monument: The Temple of Asclepius - the Hospital

The hospital is far from the center of the town of Delos, on the south western shore facing the isle of Rhenia. It is a long walk from the Delos port, and it is difficult to get to and come back from in a one day tour between boats from Mykonos. It is beside the most beautiful beach of the island, a crescent white beach in a protected cove with the mountains behind it. When you arrive at this temple, you can see the floor of the temple and the altar and rooms around it.

The role of the hospital in Delos was healing in a broad sense. People would go to the hospital because they needed the attention of the healer god. They could go if they were in need of a well-being treatment like a spa, if they were getting in shape, if they needed minor operations, or if they were preparing in a painless way, departure and passage to death.

The hospital in Delos is the temple of the gods of healing. The temple was situated in the most beautiful place on the island. In

this way, the hospital in Delos was a hospital of the future, with art, spiritual healing, a beautiful environment, temples, marble, and the sea. It was a combination of a beach resort and a spiritual healing temple. It was a combination of a spa, a hospital, a hospice, and a holistic healing center. We have not reached this level yet in hospital design or in spiritual healing technology. In this hospital there was a famous restaurant to change/regulate the diet, a place of offerings of special healing foods to the god, and consequently consumed by the patients. There was sea water bathing and purifications. There was surgery for wounds and herbs to heal. It was a place to take care of health. In the hospital people would have a great time on the beach and would also bathe, and heal with sea water.

In the temples/hospitals of Asclepius all over ancient Greece, a usual healing practice was incubation. Incubation healing was a process which involved directed dreaming in a sacred place. The sleep they went into was controlled, it was programmed by suggestion, potions, preparation; they were taught to have a dream, remember it when they woke up, and then handle it when they were awake. When they were asleep, they were even taught to have lucid dreams where they could act with intention in the dream. This process had three stages: relaxation, learning to deal with dreams, and conscious dreaming when asleep. We cannot exclude the use of mind altering or medicinal drugs; we do not know exactly what they were because the knowledge was esoteric and the secrets were not made public. For incubation, the person needed to be completely relaxed, well fed, and entertained to become calm and happy.

In incubation healing, a person would spend the night in a special room next to the temple and sleep and dream. She would first be prepared by doctors of Asclepius. In the dream, the god Asclepius would come in the night, in visions or dreams... as the god, or as a snake, and heal her. Sometimes the dream would need interpretation, and there was a priest to interpret the dream in the morning. The healing was a spiritual incubation, a prayer and a dreamtime of deep body, mind, and spirit healing.

The hospital was placed on the coast nearest the isle of Rhenia across the water where the cemetery was. When a person was in the hospital, he could see the cemetery across the water. This prepared one to choose either to die and be taken to Rhenia or to work on his healing process and stay alive in Delos. In the hospital, people saw their situation in their consciousness clearly and thus were required to do what was needed to get past the illness or give up consciously. In this way, this hospital was a portal, a gateway of life and death.

This is an artist's rendering of the moment of the boat crossing from the hospital to the cemetery on Rhenia. It shows the point of view of a patient seeing a beloved friend, seeing a person he knew a while ago taken away... and inciting himself to make the right final decision to be healed or die.

The Myth Behind the Place

Asclepius was the god of medicine and healing in ancient Greece. He had five daughters, Hygieia ("health"), Iaso ("Medicine"), Aceso ("Healing"), Aglæa/Ægle ("Healthy Glow"), and Panacea ("Universal Remedy").

His symbol was a snake twisting around his staff, and this is still the symbol of medicine today. Asclepius was a son of Apollo who gave him the gift of medicine and sent him to a centaur called Cheiron who taught him the medicinal plants. Asclepius means "cut open" in Greek because his mother, a human, died and Apollo cut him from her dead body to save him before she was cremated.

Asclepius could bring people back from the dead, and was killed by Zeus, king of the gods, because raising the dead upset the balance of life and death. Some myths say the brother of Zeus, Hades the king of the underworld, became upset, and other myths say he was killed for taking money for raising the dead.

The snake was associated with Asclepius and was used in healing ceremony. Snakes were often in the temples of Asclepius. Non-poisonous serpents were allowed to crawl on the floor, and serpents were portrayed on marble carvings in the temples above the sleeping person, along with the god. They appeared to people in healing dreams representing the god coming to heal them. The serpent as the power animal of Asclepius, god of healing, is an important ancient symbol. Serpents stood for resurrection, because they shed their skin; for life and death, because some were poisonous; and for visions because the toxin could create hallucinations when taken in low doses.

The History of the Place

Starting around 400 B.C., a cult of Asclepius grew and became popular in ancient Greece, and people came to his temples (Asclepieia) for healing. At the same time in these sanctuaries the foundation of modern medicine was established. First there would be a ritual purification, next there were offerings to Asclepius, then the person would sleep in a special sacred room called the Abaton, god's place, for incubation healing. The dream was then told to a special healing priest who would interpret the vision and tell the person what to do, what treatment or therapy was symbolically prescribed. The priests also would use love potions and incantations. The combination of dreams, visions, love potions, and incantations make Asclepius powerful and a spiritual healer. One of his early priests was Hippocrates, whom we call the father of medicine.

What To Do Here: Ceremony

The hospital is very difficult to get to, and you need to engage a tour guide. To get there, you need to follow the coast and continue south until you see a beautiful bay. The temple is on the cape of the bay facing Rhenia, the island opposite.

Close to the sea there were two big buildings where the patients were staying. Large parts of these buildings are now under the sea level which has risen since ancient times. North of these buildings there was the restaurant and finally the temple with its entrance to the east. Inside the temple there was the statue of the god wearing a golden crown and many votive offerings and gifts by the cured. There were also inscriptions and paintings describing the cures the god performed.

When you arrive at the hospital, you can go to the temple of Asclepius and pray to Asclepius, the god of healing. You can pray to heal, to be healed, or to be a healer. Ask what to do to heal. You can see this ancient hospital as an ancient place of profound spiritual healing. If you have an illness or know someone who is ill, be conscious of that healing. You can imagine being there, you can look at Rhenia or choose life actions in your life right now. You can then go swimming at the beautiful beach, be purified, and see your life as it is in this moment, beautiful and sacred.

The Words for Healing and Hospital:

Natural Vigor - the desired result of healing at the hospital
Aroma - aromatic oils, flowers, the sea, food
Ambrosial Sensations - is the smell of nature around you
Floral Essence - prepared from flowers to heal body, mind, and spirit: is a feeling of well being of body, while swimming in the bay
Blooming Fullness - how you feel after being healed
Safe and Sound - is the feeling of security
Elixir - have a sip of water
Heyday - a fantastic day, the peak, the best day of your life

Chapter Twenty One *Strength*
Rhenia The Entrance and Exit of Soul
Material

Awareness: Strength

It takes strength to face birth and death. You need strength to go to and from the world beyond to the world around. To deal with birth and with death and to cross the membrane that separates the two states, you need strength. Strength comes from your ancestors in the other world and from looking directly at birth and death, not looking away. Strength is connected to Rhenia because after the purifications, Rhenia was the maternity ward and the cemetery of Delos and was thus connected to the other worlds, to birth and to death, the great reminder. Strength comes from sincere resolution, in this case to be born/ reborn or to die.

Delos with Rhenia is a powerful birth/death portal. It is about seeing birth and death and letting the ancestor spirits speak. You know about birth and death. In Delos visiting people say to us, "I have been here before," or "I have been with this energy before," or "I recognize this place in my heart." "The ancient ones of Delos call to us, it is our destiny."

Positioning Yourself on the Monument: Orienting Yourself on the Island Vis a Vis the Two Worlds, the Live World and the Other World

You have to see this in your mind. Right across from the city of Delos is another world. There are the maternity wards where people came into this world and there is a huge necropolis where the departed ones were buried. The channel between the two islands is like a river. See the setup, it appealed to the psyche of the ancient ones living in Delos. In Greek mythology, a person dies ...he or she crosses a river and goes to the other side. So in Delos/ Rhenia, we have a channel between the two islands, it has a very strong current that goes from north to south. Believe us, the current is like a river. On one side, on Delos, there is real life—temples, dances, singing, incense, merriment, hippodrome athletic events, and celebrations. But in Delos, a person's eyes were also on the huge necropolis, a funeral monument in gleaming white marbles—24 hours a day. From everywhere on Delos, one could see Rhenia. While living a miracle in Delos... one had to take into consideration the fact that in the miracle...birth and death were inherent, inevitable, and real.

For that matter, the Egyptians who lived there, for Delos traded with Egypt, told the Greeks who learned from them...that the channel was like the Nile River. On one side were the living and on the west side—the necropolis were the dead, just like in the valley of the Kings. In actual terms, on the Delos side, that of the rising Sun God, we have life, and on the other side, the western, Rhenia, we have the setting of the sun and death.

The messengers between the two cities, the city of the dead, and the city of the living, were swimmers. In fact, swimmers famous for their speed who were called "Delian swimmers" were carrying the messages across. To this day, a Delian swimmer is a very capable swimmer.

Right across the channel is the kingdom of birth and death. They can see us, we can see them, constantly reminding each one of the other, depending on which coast one stands.

Birth and Death Are Related

It is the coming and going from the spirit world to the earth world. In ancient Greece the world of the spirits was called the underworld and was clearly defined around death. The Orphic cults and followers of Pythagoras also spoke about reincarnation and birth, death, and rebirth. The Eleusinian mysteries and Dionysian mysteries also dealt with death and afterlife and rebirth.

Consciousness is now thought of by researchers as not dependent on the body or the brain. Consciousness is there before the body and after the body so it is part of the universal consciousness of pure spirit. So with this point of view, birth is coming in from spirit and death is leaving the body to return to spirit.

In this way, Rhenia is a birth-death portal to the other world, the spirit world, the underworld. Birth and death need to be re-

An artist's imaginary rendering of the view of the great cemetery on the isle of Rhenia across the channel from Delos. One could see the accumulation of innumerable sculpted tombstones. Front right, the island of Hecate goddess of magic, witchcraft, and the dark night, front left, the island of Iris, messenger of the gods and goddess of the colors of the rainbow.

garded as equals, and going across and coming back, not as a tragedy or something to be feared. They are a natural part of life, everyone is born and dies, and preparing for death while still alive is a powerful meditation and healing. Tibetans practice meditations around death and dying, help people who are dying to go across and see lights after crossing to death. They believe that there are specific visions on the other side seen by people after death. People who have had near-death experiences tell of seeing a white light, a tunnel, angels, and family. Rhenia is the place of connecting to a consciousness separate from the body, in both birth and death.

Story: A Doctor Tells about Working with Dying People

When I am with a person who is dying, I see a hole around his or her death that allows a huge energy to pass in both directions, from earth to the other side and as important from the other side back to us that are still alive. It looks to me like a vortex or whirlwind, and I can feel a lot of energy surrounding everyone.

I feel the same kind of huge energy and connection with the other side at a birth. At a good birth, I have seen everyone fall in love, we are all bonded and everyone gets very high on the energy. At a good death, I feel the same thing. I feel a lot of information coming down to everyone present and there I feel and see the possibility of huge personal growth for the person who dies and for everyone around him/her. I feel that you can get catapulted from where you are, to a lot further along, by the energy that comes across the membrane from the other side. When a person who dies becomes pure love or pure spirit before death, you can be given a gift of love or spirit. After the death, you can be able to fall in love or embody spirit. This gift comes to you from the dying person and from the situation as that person crosses the veil.

Choosing a Body and Reincarnation

Many people have dreams or visions about choosing a body. They tell about experiences of floating in an infinite space, seeing their parents below, choosing to enter, and then coming in. Mothers also tell about knowing their babies before birth, and seeing their spirits come into them. There is also research about reincarnation where children who say they are someone else when they begin to talk were interviewed and the family they claimed to be part of found. The children could tell and recognize objects from the other family, knew the names of people, and recognized places. There are many babies who seem to know more than they could by experience and people who know things they have not been taught. Of course, many religions believe in reincarnation as a basic concept. Ancient Greece had cults that believed in reincarnation and did ceremonies called Orphic or Eleusinian Mysteries for understanding death and the afterlife.

UV Light Storms and Spirits Coming and Going

UV (ultraviolet light) storms add to our knowledge about the effects of the bright white light in Delos and miracles and healing. The incredibly bright white light with its very high UV intensity on Delos is deeply healing and part of how miracles happen in Delos. There are moments in Delos where there is an extreme intensity of UV light, big discharges of UV that are not visible to our eyes. These are UV light storms. These huge discharges of white light/UV are perceived from the effect they have on the brain. For example, you are in Delos, sitting on a marble stone, it is a perfect day, there are flowers all around you, feelings of kindness and the Delos deep blue sky. All around you is the Delian white light. All of a sudden you feel as if there is a tremendous lightning, without a sound. You wake up from your reverie, you think, "What was that?" It felt like a break out of a storm, lightning, thunder, but nothing like that happened. It happened in your head. That was UV storm, that discharge gave you the switch effect in your mind, switching your worlds. You experienced a sudden change in consciousness and more, a change in disposition.

The Delos white light can be seen and experienced. At the same time since it can be seen and experienced, it does not matter if it can be measured scientifically. We don't care about international measurements and measuring systems. It does not have to be measured to be felt. You don't see it because of measurements, but you feel it. Nothing happens outside, but you think, "Oh my, oh my God, what is that feeling?" It is like a deep crack in your nervous system, like a movement of consciousness. There is a consciousness change to something else, like a door swinging open and closing.

In a particularly strong UV storm, a soul goes . . . and a soul comes. So, people think about life and death when they feel the UV storms. Their consciousness is changed to be aware of the portal between life and death and of the movement back and forth.

UV storms move south. They are not happening in the north pole. They come to Delos in the form of storms felt but not seen. When the storms are of minor intensity, they change the humor of people; when they are of major intensity, they make people think about wanting to live or wanting to die. They are consciousness changing, bringing in conceptions of wanting to be in life. They are the Light givers.

These UV storms are moving ions and cause violent agitation. They are changing the energy in a huge way. To understand this more deeply, you can imagine that on one side is our physical world, on the other the spiritual world and there is a portal, like a hole, that connects the two. To be born, we come in from the other world to our physical world through this portal, and when we die, we leave through the same portal. Rhenia is a portal like that.

The Myth Behind the Place

The gods that were important to Rhenia were Hercules, who went to the underworld and back, and Artemis, the goddess protectress of Rhenia and childbirth. Artemis could help people be born and also help people face death and go back and forth across the veil between life and death. Artemis of Delos was also the goddess to help people go across the channel.

Hercules statue from Rhenia in Mykonos museum. He was always represented naked, with a beautiful body, carrying his favorite weapon, a bat from a tree branch and the hide from a lion that he killed which he used as his armor and mantle.

Hercules went to the underworld having in his mind, the task to tame Cerberus, a horrifying monster (a dog with three heads, or "hell hound" with a serpent's tail, a mane of snakes, and a lion's claws) who was guarding the entrance between the two worlds, not allowing communication between the living and dead. The battle between Hercules and Cerberus had to follow the rule that no weapon would be used. It would be a body combat. Hercules won and he entered the underworld and while there, he freed many who came back to the world of living. He then took Cerberus on a leash and came back, and ever since then, Hercules became a symbol of immortality. He was a human being who became a demigod and then immortal, thus overriding the limitations of the human nature. His passage to the underworld banished the notions of separate worlds and gave people a change of understanding of the underworld. He was the guarantor of the limits of human nature and the world order. As a last act to this story, he took back Cerberus to his old post and gave him his old job back because he was scaring people. Hercules finally was the one who was able to win over old age and death, and he was always considered a helper against the feeling of the horror of death.

The History of the Place

Delos was the jewel from every aspect. It had the sanctuary, the diversion, the business, the banks, the traffic—all the major powers wanted to be in control of the place from early times. Samos, Naxos, Athens, the Macedonian kings, Rome, everyone wanted to control rich Delos; as a rule, he who controlled Delos had on his side God and Money. There was no better political situation.

So when the Athenians were strong enough and wanted to solidify their hold on Delos, solidify their hold on commerce in the Aegean Sea, solidify their military hold on other islands, and take all the money in Delos and the possibility of money making in Delos—they tried to colonize it. They succeeded by using a very old myth saying that the Delians were profane. So . . . they cleansed the place more than once by removing the graves of the dead and starting in 540 B.C., moving them to a cemetery in Rhenia. They probably continued to expand an old cemetery that existed there before, now declaring it the new cemetery of the community of Delos.

Then a law was passed that no birth and no death could take place on Delos... so it would remain pure since god Apollo hated death. That stopped the creation of new Delian citizens and, maybe most importantly, stopped any claims of controlling any public or sacred property and money. Thus, with a myth of sacred and profane, they took Delos over unjustly. So, by the purifications of Delos, Athens colonized an important commercial, financial, and religious hub and used it as an asset for the advancement of its political and economic future. This also changed the spiritual connection of life and death and the gods on Delos. When people were buried near the birthplace of Apollo and Artemis, they were somehow connected to them; when they were taken to Rhenia, the connection was broken and now it was separate. Delos was no longer the homeland, and there were no citizens to claim the management of the treasures of the gods.

There were actually three cleansings in a period of a hundred years. The third one (428 B.C.) was big, and all the graves on Delos were opened, and everything taken to Rhenia and put neatly and orderly (=respectfully) in a big pit, the pit of purification. The objects and ceramics from this pit can be seen today in the Archaeological Museum of Mykonos, after they were excavated in 1906. The maternity wards were on Rhenia too, but they have not been identified yet. In fact, Rhenia is a great uncharted archaeological site that belongs to the future generations of archaeology and historical erudition.

From the moment you are in Rhenia, you are connected to the energies of birth and death. You are in that world—you start to handle your own birth and death and the birth and death of family members. This is important to be able to greet the newborns and to grieve and recover —this requires strength. There is a powerful feeling of energy that is around birth and death and a feeling of having been there before. You come here to feel that memory of births, of deaths, which is strong in you—that is the miracle of Rhenia.

What To Do Here: Ceremony

You can go to Rhenia by private boat and anchor in a bay and see the island. You can also go the museum on Mykonos and see the tombstones and ceramics from the purification pit in Rhenia where the findings from the graves were moved. In the museum, you can do ceremony to finish your day, or you can do ceremony when you get back to Mykonos. You can also see Rhenia from Delos and do ceremony towards it in the main square using as a ceremony offering tables the altars with the garlanded bulls heads that are to be seen on the square by the port.

Listening to Rhenia

From Delos, you can see Rhenia, you can see her from everywhere. You can look at Rhenia, know what she is, and listen to her from Delos. She can see you, you can see her.

Grave stone from the cemetery of Rhenia, showing a goodbye scene from the Museum of Mykonos

Altars decorated with bull's head on the square by the port. On these altars, people were performing rites to honor their dead beloved ones who were buried across the channel in the isle of Rhenia.

This was the way the ancients honored their dead when they could not go across to the cemetery on Rhenia. This was a fresco fragment from that time. The altar is in the center.

An Imaginary Trip to Rhenia...

You can picture a trip to Rhenia in your mind's eye:

Rhenia's first message is pay attention. It's hot, windy, there are no paths, only rocks in huge disorganized debris piles. Then, feel a shift, you feel the incredible energy of birth, death, and rebirth, of spirits and the underworld. And...You listen to thoughts.

They say, "Listen to us- we speak from the other side, we speak as your ancestors, we tell you of our lives. We tell you to live now, to love now. We tell you to love your children, don't make a mess. We speak as babies waiting to come, as your babies who have come to you from the other side, call them and welcome them as sacred."

And you realize your thoughts and listening to the ancient ones, the spirits of Rhenia, it's deep, wild, and powerful.

They speak a personal story to you; like in Delos, they might say, "Come here with protection, don't come alone, it can be dangerous. Come here with protection and prayer—to come across the veil to the underworld."

Rhenia is an immense portal to the other world, to the other side. Can you feel its energy? You can feel it from Delos. On Rhenia it is almost unbearable.

The Words For Birth And Death In Rhenia:

Action - the process of birth and of dying is all very active

Dynamic - all about change is dynamic, coming and going is dynamic

Strength - The other world is a great reminder, you need strength to go from the underworld to over world, to deal with birth or death, you need strength like Hercules.

Irresistible - children are intrigued by birth and by death

Invincibility - you are invincible, in life you can't die, and in death you are invincible.

Kind Force - the correct way to die and in the correct time

Succor and Stamina - relief over long time, people helping during labor and people helping in hospice

Virtue and Gallantry - necessary for birth and death, for helpers, midwives, and death aides

Vitality Preciousness - of the first and the last moment, it enhances vitality

Vitality Preciousness - of the first and the last moment, it enhances vitality

Magnanimity - unconditional generosity

Golden Vitality - the quality of light is golden in Rhenia, white in Delos

Rhenia is the Island of Birth and Death.

This amazing island that looks like
an hourglass has been the ancient
world's gateway into life and into
death.

It is one of Greece's till now
unknown islands, right in the middle
of the Aegean Sea; it is laden with
unexplored monuments from its rich
historical past that starts from the dawn of
European culture until the recent times.

The ancient historian Thucydides presents it to us as
the island where people were going to die and where
mothers would go and give birth. Its Northern
(upper) part is where the maternity wards were.
In the Southern (lower) part we have large
areas of extensive cemeteries. In the ancient
religion Rhenia has been called the "Island of
Eileithyia and Pluto" (Eileithyia is the goddess
of childbirth and Pluto god of the underworld and afterlife). People lived
on Rhenia during the first and last days of their life; here they were born
and died, it was the place of their first greeting and last bidding farewell
to the sun god Apollo and to the moon goddess Artemis.

We are working on our next project, a book about how to use the
powerful portal of Rhenia to see into birth and death. We expect with our
studies to deepen and sharpen our awareness and understanding of it.

The ancient people were visiting Rhenia as pilgrims. They were
performing rites and making offerings with the purpose of establishing
a strong sentimental and spiritual contact with their departed beloved
ones and with the beloved that were to come. On top of that they were
understanding and calculating the infinity of their existence.

It is always a matter of time and we can always turn the hourglass
around.

SECTION FOUR:

The Lessons of Delos

Chapter Twenty Two
Delos Collapses Time

Delos was a hub of transportation and communication in every sense of the word: every language, every merchandise moved there. Delos is highly understandable to us because it was a place where the architecture, mathematics, beauty, art, and sculpture, of Western Civilization was advanced and propagated. Delos is truly our ancestors speaking to us, it resonates our spiritual and cultural DNA. The triangular pediments, porticos, and columns of its buildings are the same ones we see in our capitals today all over the western world. Its beauty is the beauty we resonate with, that makes us feel good. Delos was destroyed, but in its destruction are many lessons.

Delos is now a ruin, an archaeological site. It is an out of this world place of marble stones, a place where your experience is mostly up to you. Because nothing much is left in its original form, it is a place of imagination, a place about understanding and manipulating time. That's why its history is important. When you see a statue from the 3rd century B.C. and another from the 6th century B.C. right next to it, time collapses, this cultivates your imagination. It throws you back into your deepest self. The city was destroyed and gradually abandoned and no new city was built. Delos is an opportunity to see a millennium of human energy that created a sacred society and its monuments and then see the weeds take it over. In Delos, time and space come apart and are not linear and are no longer based on logical cause and effect. Then, something magical happens to your consciousness. You open and go into the place of miracles, becoming an oracle, and seeing who you deeply are.

The name Delos means "to become apparent or outstanding" in Greek. Consequently, Delos makes you apparent as well. You see and know thyself in its bright light and incredible energy. That is consciousness; consciousness of one's self and consciousness of being social and being in nature; these things are realized in Delos.

Apollo was the god of consciousness and consciousness is high light.

Now, in destruction, Delos is even more powerful. It is a time machine. In flashbacks, you go back and forth through time. First, you see the beauty and passion in the art, then the destruction, then in a daydream, your own house, then your passion, then your own death and the death of your own city. You can swallow a thousand years in a moment, Delos is time travel. This back and forth movement is like hypnosis, it confuses and finally brings on delta brain waves and visions and peak spiritual experience. So, the destruction is part of its beneficial effect on you, it is your immediate medicine. Now, you feel the same things in your imagination and also feel the destruction. Delos as a ruin spiritually balances you with this magical consciousness expansion. It is truly a magical place of power. You are thrown into your own intuitive, creative, artistic self and find yourself in harmony, resonating with the cosmos.

A message of the ruin of Delos is, "Yes…you have the power to heal yourself." You have the power to heal others in loving them, by loving somebody else you actually love yourself…and this is the love that heals the world. With this wisdom, we have the power to heal the world, each other, and ourselves. In this book, this will be the message for self-healing…and inside that message, the secret is how to heal the world. In the ruin, Delos talks to you and tells you this. Delos is an island touchstone where all souls are uplifted and enlightened.

9/11 Happened Before

Delos, in the peak of material luxury and financial power, was destroyed in one day. Terrorists came and killed 20,000 people and took 20,000 more as slaves and pillaged the arts. They burned the buildings, took the sculptures and treasures, and left a desolated place.

Like 9/11, the rich, materialistic, luxurious island city ended in a huge act of terrorism. A terrorist act with a nuclear weapon could do the same to any of our cities in one day today. The island city was destroyed, abandoned and left to nature. The spider's web was destroyed and no one knew how to make it again. The beauty, spirituality, and healing of this city has never been equaled. Delos, the apparent one, became A-delos the dis-apparent again. This lesson of destruction of a culture that had lost the balance of its spiritual base is fundamental to our lives. Balance is necessary, it is the lesson of Apollo, of Delos to us today. The destruction of Delos changed the world history. What can we learn from this story?

The curative elements that made Delos a healing and spiritually balancing place are deeply pertinent to our lives now. In Delos, spiritual life, financial life, art, music, dance, song, and ceremony were united to make a culture that was a paradigm for the whole ancient world. The healing ceremony and culture of Delos was imitated and taught everywhere, as far as the Black Sea countries, and as far away as France. Delos was the model for the world in spiritual healing technology. When the culture became too materialistic and political, it collapsed and was destroyed as a symbol and as a reality. Our culture is in jeopardy today; there are forces that make it unstable and cause financial, health, and spiritual crises. People are hungry for change.

This story is a powerful contemporary life lesson. Today, we need balance, we need to have both the spiritual and the material to have a healthy society that can endure through time by evolution and advancement. We need to know how to create a society that constantly heals in balance with material growth.

The Delian Problem

Delos has many lessons for us today. Delos had an ancient story of how illness and poverty acted to heal a whole culture. The lesson was called The Delian Problem. Once there was a plague in Delos. It killed many people and was a huge health problem. So, the people asked the oracle of Apollo what to do. The oracle gave them a problem to solve and said if they solved it the plague would end. The oracle asked them to double the volume of the altar of the horns in front of the temple of Apollo, the most important monument in Delos. The solution was not solvable with the compass and the ruler or with any two dimensional thinking that was in use until that time. Its eventual mathematical solution resulted in the first three dimensional geometry and stereometry. This was a major step in human consciousness. The people of Delos later made mosaics using the three dimensional perspective that looked like modern M. C. Escher art. This was an example of an illness, a social calamity leading to huge progress in mathematics, geometry, and art. The plague ended when the problem was solved with the new methods. Consciousness, the gift of Apollo, is the high tech of thinking. The Delian problem is one of the symbols of consciousness. One of the most important lessons from Delos is that the Delian problem can be applied to all. It's about finding a dramatic new way of looking at the world—finding a better, larger way. That is the lesson of Delos, we can't look at things in old ways anymore. It's clearly not working. It is an emblematic way of approaching any problem; take it in, live with it, and create a dimension in your way of thinking that includes your new world.

This is a great teaching for our society. We have many illnesses in our culture. They are due to war, poverty, huge differences in wealth, environmental problems, population growth—these are toxic situations. To solve these problems we have to add them as an extra dimension in our existence and live with them and their consequences until we learn them and tackle them. In terms of Delos, toxic means deadly from Apollo's favorite weapon, the toxon=bow. Apollo was a punishing god for trespassers. His lesson was, get rid of the toxins that cause illnesses, personal and cultural. For our culture, the plague illness, it is war, it is poverty, it is hunger, it is malaria. When we go to the oracle, she tells us we need a new way of thinking, our Delian problem is to think out of the box. It was hard in Delos with increasing wealth and power, and it's hard now with greed and power.

Delos calls to us now to reconsider our culture and change the world. Truly, Delos is a huge lesson in changing global values. Now we have a culture that is reeling in greed and gross materialism. Other cultures are being destroyed by the opposite, by spiritual excesses justifying terrorism and war.

If we could balance spiritual and material values, this would be healing to the earth, cultures, and health. The teachings of Delos are about what is real truth. The teachings are about what is balance.

What were the classical values, how can we balance spiritual and material life, and what are ethical truths? This was the teaching of ancient Greece as much as were the triangular pediments and porticos and columns of the marble buildings. The lesson of Delos is to prepare the next generation on how to live.

Mykonos is taken in by pleasure, drugs, alcohol, luxury goods, and conspicuous consumption on a world class scale. Less than 30 years ago, it was a natural island with fisherman and farmers and the change came quickly and violently. Each day, people who go from Mykonos to Delos are reminded graphically of what happens when materialism and wealth get out of balance with spiritual values.

The Gift of This Book

This book will give you a precious gift, something to take with you, for your lives. It will give you a precious gift from ancient Delos: like an ancient ball of knowledge. The ball of knowledge is like a ball of light, the light of Apollo. The ancient Greeks believed that the light of Apollo was special, it was a pure white light with no rainbow shades of color in it.

The ribbon on the top of the gift of Delos is the surprise. It comes from the mystery of the pure white light. The surprise is that you can realize that, " I am here and it is perfect. I have evolved beyond this ruin now and I know all this… in this moment, in a flash, I can know myself and solve my life problems." You become smarter than the whole scenario, the book makes you feel 5000 years smarter. The mystery is that you find that you are given the gift of knowing what has been unreachable is now yours. The deepest secrets of the ancient Greeks are now accessible, the deepest philosophy of light and consciousness is now inside you.

Understanding Delos will give you an understanding of yourself. You can take this ball of light and in difficult times recall knowledge and understanding of your deeper self. You become your own oracle. That was the gift of Apollo, of Delos throughout history. The intense white light engulfs you, protects you, and covers you like a blanket.

The Fourth Dimension in Delos

Delos is moving into the fourth dimension. Delos was the place where 3D was discovered with the solution to the Delian problem, and now it is a place for 4D. We usually view our world from the outdated Delian perspective, which looks at space as consisting of three dimensions, and time as one dimension. The "fourth dimension," 4D is all the dimensions plus time. In this 4D view of the world, spacetime is a model that merges space and time into a single interwoven continuum, spacetime just like Delos.

Spacetime joins space and time to a single concept. Normally, in our thinking, there are three space dimensions (length, width, height), and one time dimension (time). Each of these are necessary to locate a point in space. For example, on the earth, the latitude and longitude both determine a point in space. In spacetime, the points that contain the 3+1 dimensions locate events (not just points in space). In this model, time as another dimension adds to the coordinates. In this way the coordinate points determine where and when events occur.

Delos does this by being in the beginning of history and moving to the future. Delos covers a span of 6000 years before now, and it is entering a span of 6000 years ahead. For this new dimension of 4D, Delos is spacetime becoming a reality.

If you can stand in the ruins of an entire civilization—3000 or 6000 years in development—pushed up to its quintessential peak of divine light, of oracular power, of spiritual healing—then annihilated in a bloodbath of aggression; and you can forgive ALL the passions involved, encompass and embody ALL those voices raised in prayer and ecstasy for centuries—you will become unmoored and liberated from your tiny, isolated, miniscule island in time and space. You will become so expanded, so all encompassing, so exalted—that your life of obstacles, obligations, and inexactitudes will be instantly and irrevocably dissolved and joined with the vast, harmonious opera of the cosmic spheres.

We live both at the same time, we live time past and time present simultaneously. We are our very own future now. That is the gift of Delos as of now and for the future. We want this book to be more than a visit, we want it to be the experience that is coming to change your life. We want this book and Delos to be the place of a miracle for you.

Appendix One:

A Special Sacred Visit to the the Synagogue of Delos

A Story of the Woman Who Did a Ceremony to Cure Her Husband and Keep Him Alive

She had tears in her eyes when she asked George to take her to the synagogue in Delos. She was a Jewish woman from New York whose dear husband, whom she loved, had just been diagnosed with terminal cancer. His doctor had told him he would only live a short time and to get his affairs in order. But, his beautiful wife had other ideas. She had read that there was a ruin of marble stones on the archaeological site of Delos that was the oldest synagogue in the world outside of Jerusalem, and she knew exactly what she wanted to do. She wanted to go the this ancient Jewish sacred site and make a miracle. George Voulgaris was her guide, and he took her to the site. They walked together in the hot sun, for a half hour. They even climbed over walls and went down rarely used dirt paths. The site was far away from the main excavation and far from the main visit paths. When she arrived she saw that because it was remote the site was littered with all sorts of packaging trash left there over a long period from random previous visitors. The place was also full of overgrown thorny bushes and thistles. She went immediately to work with intense fervor, cleaning the whole place with her bare bleeding hands in two hours. She wanted it purified and sacred for what she had in mind. She stood first in the center of what was the big room and said a prayer. "Father, King of the Universe, I pray to you to let me into your sacred temple for healing." She then walked to the beautiful marble throne in the main hall of the synagogue. She spoke to the spirits of the ancient rabbis who were using the throne, " I ask you to pray for my husband. He is a lovely man who helps people wherever he goes. He is ill now and needs your prayers." The rabbis said, "Thank you for coming to our ancient temple sacred woman. It was our sacred synagogue, away from home for many many years. Thank you for waking it up now. You can do a ceremony here for your husband and I and we shall all pray for him." So the woman took flowers, and placed them around the site, and *poured some water from her drinking bottle in the site of the ancient mikvah, the ancient purification baths, and she prayed the sacred Jewish prayer for healing. "May the one who blessed our ancestors, Abraham, Isaac and Jacob, Sarah, Rebecca, Rachel and Leah, bless and heal my husband who is ill . May the Blessed Holy One be filled with compassion for his health to be restored and his strength to be revived. May God swiftly send him a complete renewal of body and spirit, and let us say, Amen." Then, she heard a voice. "Your husband will be well, woman. Celebrate and go." She took out her bagels and lox, chopped liver and gefilte fish, which she brought to honor her ancestors, and shared her food with George. And they left.*

Her husband did not die like the doctor had said. In fact, he lived many, many, years and died of old age. The prayers to the Father on the ancient site of the synagogue on Delos had cured him. She got a special miracle on Delos, the Island of Miracles.

History of the Place

The synagogue of Delos may be the oldest synagogue in the world. Built between 150 and 128 B.C.E., it was used until the second century A.D.

The synagogue was discovered in 1912. The fact that this building was a Jewish synagogue relies on an inscription found in stone, "Theos Hypsistos," or "God Most High," which applied to the Jewish God, and relies also on the Jewish arrangement and layout of the rooms, benches, and seats which indicate a public building and are not like an ordinary dwelling.

The monument is on the east side of Delos, far away from the center of the city in a residential area where have been excavated so far a large school, shops, a stadium, a perfumer's workshop, and grounds for the extraction of the porphyry dye from seashells by the seashore. It is above a beautiful beach that is protected from the wind. The synagogue had two large rooms, a beautiful marble throne, and many marble benches. It also had a room with access by descending steps to a water reservoir that could have been used as a Mikvah, a Jewish ritual bath. All these characteristics are not consistent with those of a private house, a meeting place for an association, or a Greek cult building, but rather confirm its function as a synagogue from the earliest phase onward.

Many people wonder whether Apostle Paul passed by Delos. We know he visited the Jewish communities of the pagan world. Delos had a large Jewish community and this synagogue. If Paul was crisscrossing the Aegean, what makes us think that he could not have been in Delos as well? Definitely, however, we do not have a letter written by Paul to the Delians.

Ceremony, What You Can Do Here

If you wish, you can do a special pilgrimage to this ancient monument. You need to ask your guide to take you there since it is away from the main site and not on any usual tour. Like the beautiful woman in the story above, you can do a ceremony here for healing, for life change, for miracles, and for transformation. Like her, you can bring some food to celebrate, and say prayers to the throne of the rabbis, put water from a water bottle in the mikvah purification baths (you can't go down in the water now). The traditional Jewish prayer for healing is: "Blessed are You, LORD our God, King of the Universe, Who bestows good things upon the unworthy, and has bestowed upon me every goodness."

At the mikvah you are cleansed and purified from head to toe. In between your fingers underneath your nails. Inside your ears. all the hard-to-reach places and neglected places are attended to. Here you are cleansed on a physical level, on an emotional level, on a mental level, and on a spiritual level.

Be sure to clean up the site when you leave. Don't leave any trace of your ceremony. Let the voices of the ancient rabbis talk to you, let your heart open and pray there, in the oldest Jewish place of prayer in the diaspora.

1. Ask your guide to take you to the Jewish synagogue
2. Pray to ancestors to enter
3. When you enter, talk in front of the throne to the endless line of ancient rabbis who were sitting there. Go to the mikvah baths and do your purification with water, and sit on the benches and pray.

4. Say your prayers, in a way that is good for you for healing, miracles, oracle, and transformation of your life.

Here Are Traditional Jewish Prayers for Healing:

May the One who blessed our ancestors Abraham, Isaac, and Jacob, Sarah, Rebecca, Rachel and Leah, bless and heal the one who is ill: [*put the name here*] son/daughter of [*name*].

May the Holy One, the fount of blessings, shower abundant mercies upon him/her, fulfilling his/her dreams of healing, strengthening him/her with the power of life.

Merciful one, restore him/her, heal him/her, strengthen him/her, enliven him/her. Send him/her a complete healing from the heavenly realm, a healing of body and a healing of soul, together with all who are ill soon, speedily, without delay; and let us say: Amen!

Throne of the rabbis, in the Synagogue of Delos

Appendix Two

Orientation: The Mykonos Archipelago

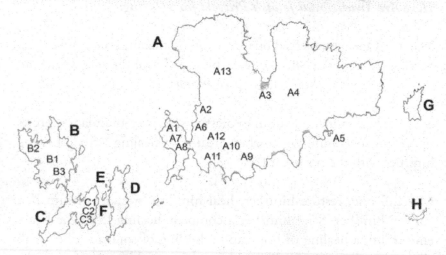

Map Key

A Mykonos Island

A1 The Peninsula of Kanalia possibly the Lost island of
Ortygia. This peninsula used to be a separate island from
Mykonos some seven thousand years ago. Wind and rain
erosion of the coastal lands along with the strong sea cur-
rents formed a bank of sand that united the two islands.
On that bank of sand is built the modern village of Ornos.

Ortygia is the name an island known to us from the
myths. It is referred as the sacred island of Goddess
Artemis next to Delos where she would go hunting but
it was unidentifiable until recently. Ortygia means the
Island of Quails and indeed the quail was the goddess'
sacred bird and the particular peninsula still is a stopover
of the migrating quails. On it we have the remnants of
an organized settlement as of 5000 B.C.

A2 The town of Mykonos. Site of the oldest settlement on the
island inhabited until today (8000 years B.C. and possibly
older).

A3 The stone age settlement in the bay of Ftelia. From 5000 B.C.

A4 The Fortified hill of Palaiokastro. The remnants of a very old community living on a fortified hilltop. At the foot of the hill there are still two "menhirs," i.e., sacred monolithic stone columns testaments of the existence of organized community on the island in the very far past (10 000 B.C.)

A5 The peninsula of the two breasts or Divounia, the area of the earliest organized settlement of Mykonos (8000 years B.C. and possibly older)

A6 The remnants of the beehive grave of the pre-historical king of Mykonos. Homer calls him Ajax of Lokro

A7 Excavations of a stoneage settlement

A8 Cemetery of the same period

A9 A ship observation castle at the location called Pyrgi

A10 A deep well for drinking water that dates from 2000 years B.C. One would go down to the water level with steps

A11 Another enemy ship observation castle at a location called Portes

A12 Remnant of a fortified palace at the valley of Lino

A13 Ruins of a possible temple of Apollo from 600 Years B.C.

B North Rhenia Island

B1 Remnants of the medieval Castle of the Knights of St John.

B2 Ruins of the ancient city of Rhenia and its harbor.

B3 Ruins of possibly the ancient maternity wards of Rhenia.

C South Rhenia Island

C1 The Great Cemetery

C2 The vothros (=pit) of the Catharsis where all the graves from Delos were moved to.

C3 Temple of Hercules

D Delos Island

E Small Revmatiaris Island or the Island of Hekate, goddess of the dark night, Magic and witchcraft.

F   Large Revmatiaris Island or *The Island of Iris*, goddess of the rainbow colors and messenger of the gods.

G   Tragonisi or Goat's Island

H   Stapodia Islands

The Islands of the Mykonos Archipelago

These islands are situated in the center of the Aegean Sea, midway between the mainland of Greece and the coast of Asia Minor. They are part and they are in the middle of a larger group of islands called the Cyclades. This name comes from the circular shape that this group of islands form, ('cyclo' in Greek). Many of these islands are small and uninhabited and are used mainly as grazing grounds by the inhabitants of the larger islands which have been inhabited since the depths of history.

Mykonos is the largest of the group. Inhabited with approx 10,000 people.

Rhenia second in size, is divided into two parts, North and South, by a narrow strip of land. It is not inhabited now and is used as grazing grounds and small agriculture patches by the inhabitants of Mykonos. It is an island full with the ruins of its important past that has not been archaeologically and historically studied yet.

Delos is one of the smaller islands. Its approximate size is 6.5 sq. kilometers. It is 1.3 kilometers wide, by about 5km long. Delos too, has been inhabited from time immemorial, and on it developed a large, thriving city.

Before any other consideration, Delos must be seen in relation to the other cycladic islands around her, Mykonos and especially Rhenia. From Mykonos, Delos is five nautical miles away. Rhenia is just across from the western coast of Delos, the two islands forming a channel less than one km wide.

In the middle of the channel there are two very tiny islands called the two Revmatiaris islands (Revmatiaris means roughly in Greek 'the island on the current channel'). Indeed there is a current in the channel going North to South. This channel, along with the two little islands in the middle, apparently was very important in the transformation of a tiny island like Delos into a safe port.

Remember that Delos, being in the center of the Aegean, is situated at the meeting point of all the important trade routes of this sea, from North to South and especially from west (Greek mainland) to the East (Asia Minor). This busy spot of the Aegean also is one of the most difficult to navigate, because all summer long (and let us not forget that summer was the navigational season in the old times when there were no motorboats), the local North wind (Meltemi) can make the sea extremely rough for several days. So, it was inevitable that an important port and not just a shelter should be available, midway. Delos, forming together with Rhenia a rather quiet channel and having the ports of its Western side protected by the two small Revmatiaris islands, was the best place for early seafarers to stop for a few days, provide their ships with fresh water, exchange information with other seafarers, and wait for the sea to calm down, or just to stop over midway between their departure point and their destination. Then, as now, it took two days to cross the Aegean by sail.

Geologically, the island is just like the rest of the Cyclades, consisting mainly of schist and granite. This makes the soil very poor; moreover, the whole terrain of Delos is taken up by several extremely rocky hills, the highest of which is Mt. Cynthus (112m). What little soil remains is continually being washed down to the sea by the winter rain torrents. The only cultivable part is a small plain near the main port, and that was occupied by the buildings of the ancient Sanctuary. Moreover, schist and granite are very hard stones, impenetrable by water, and make impossible the formation of any water springs. In fact, what little fresh water there is on the island is due to a few limestone deposits and some large natural bowls of granite. (The rainwater is absorbed by the limestone, filtered, and kept in the bowl. Thus, by digging a well in the limestone, one gets naturally filtered and very tasty fresh water.)

We should call the climate of Delos an Aegean-island climate: that is to say, very mild winters, no snow, but chilly January and February; a glorious spring, summer and fall. The temperature can be high in summer, but never unbearable because of the summer winds that blow over the Aegean from the North, going towards the African desert to fill there the vacuum that the desert's hot air leaves as it goes upwards. We could safely say that the sun shines on Delos 300 days in a year. It rains only in winter time, and the annual rainfall is about 400 millimeters. The best time to visit Delos is spring and fall, particularly spring, when the wildflowers are in bloom. The coastline (about 13 Kilometers) is very rocky and indented. On Delos there are only two sandy spots: the bay of Fourni and Skardana. Rhenia offers wonderful beaches all around its coast, but it has a less easy access.

Tragonisi or Goat's island. Not inhabited but indeed there are a lot of goats grazing on it.

Stapodia Islands. Not inhabited, great fishing grounds and on it ancient murex shell culture beds. From these shells ancient people were extracting the porphyry pigment, or the purple dye.

Practical Advice and Rules While in Delos.

Delos happens to be a special island: it is now considered a museum, a monument to be revered, it is not a playground, although it is qualified for it. So the island is closely guarded. There are guards who keep it up, and you must always obey their comments. They have the authority to remove you. The island is a Government property.

You must take the utmost care of the ruins. Do not further ruin the place, 2000 years was bad enough. Do not climb on the walls. Do not touch the ruined stuccoes. Do not take any stones for souvenirs at all. (Remember the stone you have taken is probably the missing piece of the puzzle an archaeologist is spending his life trying to solve.) Do not try to become an archaeologist by digging the soil. You destroy the archaeological strata and thus create further problems. Also do not litter. There are no waste baskets about, so retain wrappers, and the like. Soft drink bottles must not be taken away from the restaurant. There is no other place to put them; drink your drink there. When visiting the Museum, do not go wearing a bikini; it is not allowed. The guards do not like visitors who climb marble statue bases or the lions. When walking about YOU MUST ALWAYS FOLLOW THE PATHS. DO NOT GO INTO THE SHRUBS; there is the danger of a hidden cistern, or well, or a snake, etc. THERE ARE PATHS FOR YOU TO GO ANYWHERE YOU LIKE. If you are on your own and visiting certain monuments off the beaten track, make sure to watch carefully where you are stepping, as there may be a cistern below your feet ready to give away. There are only a few shaded places. The sun is merciless at any time, so take a hat and sunglasses. And wear shoes.

Make sure you know when the last boat of the day will return from Delos to Mykonos because Delos is a museum island and has closing hours and there is no facility to spend the night on the island. If you want to go to Rhenia, you must hire a boat from Mykonos.

You may take any pictures on site you like. Tripods are not permitted. Use no flash in the museum. Delos must be considered an uninhabited island. There are no accommodations. As a general rule, no one may stay on Delos overnight. Since the bottom of the sea around the island is full of antiquities, diving is not permitted.

Authors Bios

GEORGE VOULGARIS (Yori) has been educated in the USA, France, and Japan. He is a multi-linguist and has been for the past forty years luxuriating in the archaeology of Delos. He is the guide to the National Geographic teams that visit the Greek islands and Delos. His special studies on ancient metals have turned him into a jeweler. He is a Mykonos native.

DIMITRA VOULGARIS is an archaeologist from the University of Athens whose specialty is Mycenaean and Classical Greece. Her particular endeavor is the study of the bibliography on the excavations of Delos. She is a multi-linguist, and at times she presents the ruins to an international public of people with that particular interest.

MICHAEL SAMUELS, M.D. is a recognized expert in how art, sculpture, and music cause life change and healing, and has used guided imagery with patients with life-threatening illness for over 30 years. He lives on the island of Tinos, Greece, where he is sculpting marbles.

These authors have joined together to bring Delos alive because they love Delos and have experienced the healing power of Delos themselves and with many others. They will show you how you can change your life by taking you to Delos, the place of miracles.

Symbols For the Twelve Awarenesses

1. Power of Consciousness

2. Power and Grace

3. Oracular Power

4. Creation

5. Fertility

6. The Source of Life

7. Metamorphosis

8. Love

9. Protection

10. Victory

11. Health

12. Strength

International Friends of Delos - Who we are

The book is bigger than any one person. Throughout the years innumerable friends from all the four corners of the globe have been visiting Delos and been affected by its soothing and healing energy. Every one of them had something to say, sing, write, paint, definitely something to add to the body of impressions that we have collected and has become the core of this book.

We want to hope that your impressions too will be known to us, thus add to the beneficial information we try to convey. In health and in culture.

www.internationalfriendsofdelos.com

Artemis Books

To contact the publisher with retail or wholesale inquiries:

Artemis Books
P.O. Box 1108
Penn Valley, CA 95946
USA
phone: +1 (530) 277-5380
email: artemisbooks@gmail.com
web site: www.artemis-books.com